Saturday Kitchen

Digital food photography by Steve Lee

This book is based on the television series *Saturday Kitchen* produced for
BBC2 by Prospect Pictures Ltd.
Executive producer: Barry Lynch
Commissioning editor for the BBC: Dominic Vallely

Published by BBC Books, BBC Worldwide Ltd
Woodlands, 80 Wood Lane, London W12 0TT

First published 2004
Introduction © copyright Antony Worrall Thompson 2004
Recipes © copyright the contributors 2004
The moral rights of the contributors have been asserted.
Food photography by Steve Lee © copyright BBC Worldwide 2004

ISBN: 0 563 52111 2

Commissioning editor: Vivien Bowler
Project editor: Sarah Lavelle
Copy editor: Mari Roberts
Cover art director: Pene Parker
Design manager: Sarah Ponder
Designer: Lisa Pettibone
Home economist: Joss Herd
Stylist: Lucy Pearse
Photographic assistants: Paul Blundell and Tony Briscoe
Production controller: Kenneth McKay

If you require further information on any BBC Worldwide product call
08700 777 001 or visit our website on www.bbcshop.com

Set in Caecilia and Foundry Sans
Printed and bound in Italy by L.E.G.O. spa
Colour separations by Radstock Reproductions Ltd

Eggs are medium (size 3) unless otherwise specified. The chefs recom-
mend the use of free-range and/or organic eggs wherever possible.

Saturday Kitchen

Compiled and edited by Orla Broderick

With recipes from

Rosa Baden Powell
Ed Baines
Mary Berry
Celia Brooks Brown
Gennaro Contaldo
Richard Corrigan
Gino D'Acampo
Jill Dupleix
Silvana Franco
Bill Granger

Valentina Harris
Paul Hollywood
Ken Hom
Sue Lawrence
Manju Malhi
James Martin
Reshma Martin
Paul Merrett
Merrilees Parker
Thane Prince

Jeanne Rankin
Paul Rankin
Mike Robinson
Liz Scourfield
Curtis Stone
James Tanner
Tony Tobin
Mitch Tonks
Lesley Waters
Antony Worrall Thompson

BBC BOOKS

Contents

Introduction

Countdown to *Saturday Kitchen*:

Saturday morning: it's 5.00 a.m. I awake to the none-too-harmonious tones of four alarm clocks. Wandsworth is calling – Capital Studios await – but not before an uplifting cup of tea and a bracing shower. *Saturday Kitchen* here we come.

Initially it was fear; now it's the anticipation of a live TV show. *Saturday Kitchen* was pleasantly thrust upon me just weeks before my sojourn in the Australian jungle as part of *I'm a Celebrity: Get Me Out of Here!* I had no time to adjust to the rigours of presenting my first live show, but nearly a year on, I feel at ease with myself, and have a set Saturday morning routine.

6.30 a.m. sees an early breakfast read-through of scripts, adjusting the wording, and discussing the autocue. 7.00 a.m. and it's into make-up (extra eye drops for me!). 7.30 a.m. is rehearsal time and an introduction to the day's studio guests. Not many TV chefs miss the opportunity of appearing on the show. It's always a colourful line-up – including the likes of Rick Stein, Madhur Jaffrey, Ken Hom and Gino

D'Acampo – and it's fantastic for me to work alongside so many knowledgeable characters.

Rehearsals finish at about 9.30 a.m. after a full run-through, with timings practised, camera angles perfected. For a live show it is essential that the director knows every move, guests must feel comfortable with their dishes and I must know exactly what I have to do. Instructions follow through my earpiece, timings interject, and prompts on the subject in hand are always forthcoming. I have a busy right ear and the left one doesn't get away lightly as I also need to listen to my guests. There was I thinking that it was only my wife who could listen to three conversations at once!

9.30 a.m. brings a welcome 15-minute break, some 'chill-out' deep breathing and a make-up renovation before we rehearse the 'top of the show' once again. Nerves are starting to jangle, adrenalin levels are high. It's nearly that time: one last unnecessary read-through of the script, then good-luck wishes all round. It's 9.59 a.m.... 'Thirty seconds to on-air' comes through my earpiece. 10.00 a.m.... 'We're on air, twenty-one seconds on titles', and then I'm on my own – there's no going back: we're live.

'Hi, thanks for joining us. On today's show...'

Antony Worrall Thompson, *Presenter*, Saturday Kitchen

1 Apple and Onion Soup with Crumbled Stilton

JEANNE RANKIN
SOUP

Serves 6

50 g/2 oz unsalted butter

1 kg/2 lb onions, roughly chopped

2 Bramley apples

500 ml/18 fl oz medium dry cider

1 tbsp cider vinegar

pinch of dried thyme

$^1\!/_2$ bay leaf

2 litres/3$^1\!/_2$ pints chicken stock

225 g/8oz potato, peeled and diced

1 onion, thinly sliced (to use as a garnish)

75 g/3 oz Stilton

handful of fresh chervil sprigs

salt and freshly ground black pepper

This soup is a variation on the classic French onion soup and uses cider instead of white wine to deglaze the caramelized onions. The pectin in the apples helps thicken the soup as well as adding more texture. Any cheese can be used but blue cheese has a sweetness that works really well in this soup.

1 Heat a heavy-based pan over medium heat. Add half the butter, then tip in the onions and allow to cook gently for about 15 minutes, or until they are softened and lightly browned, stirring occasionally.

2 Peel the apples and remove the cores, then roughly chop and toss in a little of the cider to prevent discoloration. Deglaze the pan with the remaining cider and the cider vinegar. Add the apples and bring to the boil, then reduce the heat and simmer for about 15 minutes, or until the cider has reduced by half.

3 Add the thyme to the pan with the bay leaf, stock and potato, and season with a little salt. Bring to a simmer, then cook for another 15 minutes or until the potato is completely tender, stirring occasionally. Remove the bay leaf from the pan and whiz the soup to a purée with a hand-held blender or in batches in the food processor. Season to taste.

4 To make the garnish, heat the remaining butter in a frying pan and sauté the onion slices until softened and just beginning to colour around the edges. To serve, reheat the soup gently and ladle into warm bowls. Crumble a tablespoon of the Stilton into each bowl, and garnish with the fried onion slices and chervil sprigs.

2 Chilled Tomato Bisque

ANTONY WORRALL
THOMPSON
SOUP

Serves 4–6

1 small red pepper

1 slice country-style white bread

2 tsp sherry vinegar

1/2 garlic clove, peeled and finely chopped

1 tsp caster sugar

1/2 red chilli, seeded and finely diced

2–4 tbsp extra virgin olive oil

225 g/8 oz plum tomatoes, peeled, seeded and roughly chopped

2 tsp tomato ketchup

200 ml/7 fl oz tomato juice

2 spring onions, thinly sliced

1/2 large cucumber, peeled, seeded and roughly diced

2 tsp good-quality ready-made pesto (or home-made)

salt and freshly ground black pepper

frozen olive-oil cubes, to serve

Based on a gazpacho but smooth instead of chunky, this soup is wonderfully refreshing on a hot day. It needs to be served well chilled and in small portions, and it's worth remembering that cold food needs to be highly seasoned to bring out the best flavours. Frozen olive oil cubes are easy to make. Pour extra virgin olive oil into ice-cube moulds and freeze solid, then use as required.

1 Preheat the grill. Place the red pepper on the grill rack and cook for 20–30 minutes until well charred and blistered, turning regularly. Transfer to a polythene bag and secure with a knot. Leave to cool completely, then peel. Chop the flesh, reserving any juices and discarding the seeds and core.

2 Cut off the crusts from the bread and discard. Cut the remainder up and place in a food processor or liquidizer. With the machine running, add the vinegar, garlic, sugar and chilli and blend until smooth.

3 Add the extra virgin olive oil a little at a time to the bread until it will absorb no more. Add the roasted red pepper flesh, tomatoes, tomato ketchup, tomato juice, spring onions, cucumber and pesto. Continue to blend to form a smooth emulsion. Season to taste. Pour into a non-metallic jug and chill for at least 2 hours (or overnight is fine). To serve, season to taste and then ladle the soup into wide-rimmed bowls. Garnish with the frozen olive oil cubes.

3 Seafood Laksa

ANTONY WORRALL
THOMPSON
STARTER

Serves 6

groundnut oil, for cooking

9 baby squid, cleaned and cut into 5 cm/2 in pieces

350 g/12 oz monkfish fillet, skinned and cut into 5 cm/2 in chunks

18 raw tiger prawns, peeled and veins removed

1 large lemon, halved and pips removed

2 medium-hot red chillies, halved and seeded

4 garlic cloves, roughly chopped

5 cm/2 in piece of fresh root ginger, peeled and roughly chopped

1 tsp ground coriander

50 g/2 oz bunch of fresh coriander (including roots)

50 ml/2 fl oz toasted sesame oil

1.2 litres/2 pints coconut milk

850 ml/1½ pints fish or vegetable stock

200 g/7 oz dried vermicelli noodles

175 g/6 oz sugar snap peas

50 ml/2 fl oz Thai fish sauce (*nam pla*)

handful of fresh mint and basil leaves

3 spring onions, thinly sliced

Laksa is a Singaporean/Malaysian dish that's a real favourite of mine as it's healthy and fresh but also chilli-warming. This is the kind of thing I like to make for friends at home. Don't be put off by the list of ingredients – it is very straightforward to prepare. Essentially, it's an easy one-pot soup with 'wow' factor. Put it in the middle of the table so that everyone can help themselves.

1 Heat a griddle pan. Brush with a little oil and then chargrill the squid for 30–45 seconds on each side. Place on a plate and leave to cool, then add the monkfish and prawns. Squeeze over the lemon juice and set aside to marinate.

2 Heat a large pan. Place the chillies in a food processor with the garlic, ginger, ground coriander, fresh coriander and sesame oil, and blend into a coarse paste. Add to the heated pan and stir-fry for 1 minute, then pour in the coconut milk and stock and bring to the boil. Simmer for 10 minutes to allow the flavours to combine and until slightly reduced, stirring occasionally.

3 Place the noodles in a large pan of boiling salted water and then immediately remove it from the heat. Set aside for 3–4 minutes, depending on manufacturer's instructions, then drain and refresh under cold running water. Set aside. Blanch the sugar snap peas in a small pan of boiling salted water, drain and refresh under cold running water. Set aside.

4 Add the fish sauce to the coconut mixture with the monkfish and stir gently for just a few seconds. Add the chargrilled squid and the prawns and stir gently for another few seconds until the prawns are just cooked and opaque in colour. Place the cooked noodles in a large serving bowl and scatter the sugar snap peas on top. Ladle over the hot coconut broth and sprinkle the mint and basil leaves and the spring onions on top to serve.

4 Avocado Prawn Salad with Honey Mustard Dressing

MARY BERRY
STARTER

Serves 2

1 small, just ripe avocado

a few fresh rocket leaves

12 cooked peeled tiger prawns, about 75 g/3 oz in total

handful of seedless white grapes, halved

FOR THE DRESSING:

2 tbsp sunflower oil

1 tsp Dijon mustard

1 tbsp clear honey

1 tbsp chopped fresh dill

juice of ½ lime

salt and freshly ground black pepper

2 lime wedges and 2 large whole cooked king prawns, to garnish

warm crusty bread, to serve

This is my version of that old favourite – prawn cocktail. The sweetness of the honey in the dressing mellows the sharpness of the mustard without overpowering it. Dill may seem like an unusual choice of herb but it is used a great deal with fish and shellfish in Scandinavian cookery and is fantastic with this salad. It has a mild aniseed flavour, much more subtle than fennel. The grapes add a freshness and crunch to the salad.

1 To make the dressing, place the oil in a small bowl with the mustard, honey, dill and lime juice. Season to taste and whisk until well blended.

2 Cut the avocado in half, remove the stone and carefully scoop out the flesh in one piece. Cut each avocado half into six or seven slices and arrange on plates in a circle.

3 Put a pile of rocket on top of each circle of avocado and scatter over the tiger prawns and grapes. Season to taste and drizzle over the dressing. Garnish with the lime wedges and king prawns. Serve with the warm crusty bread.

5 Smoked Haddock Risotto with Pancetta

Serves 4

2 tbsp white wine vinegar

4 large eggs

1 tbsp olive oil

1 large shallot, finely chopped

1 tsp medium curry powder

1 tsp chopped fresh thyme

1 bay leaf

500 ml/18 fl oz fish or vegetable stock

250 g/9 oz arborio (risotto) rice

500 ml/18 fl oz milk

275 g/10 oz smoked haddock fillet (preferably un-dyed)

12 thin slices pancetta or rindless streaky bacon rashers

75 g/3 oz frozen petits pois

25 g/1 oz unsalted butter, diced and chilled

25 g/1 oz mascarpone cheese

2 tbsp chopped fresh flat-leaf parsley

½ lemon, pips removed

salt and freshly ground black pepper

The first secret to risotto success is to use a good-quality, heavy-based, shallow pan – a sauté pan is perfect. The second secret is arborio rice, a speciality rice that can take up to six times its volume in liquid, but the liquid must be added little by little, allowing each ladleful to be completely absorbed before adding the next. Enrich the risotto at the very end of cooking – such as with butter and mascarpone, as here – for a rich, smooth finish.

1 To poach the eggs, heat 2.25 litres/4 pints of water in a large pan. Add the vinegar and bring to the boil. When the water is bubbling, break the eggs one by one into the water, then reduce the heat to very low (or move the pan to the edge of the heat) and leave to simmer gently for 3 minutes. Remove each egg with a slotted spoon and plunge into a bowl of iced water. When cold, trim any ragged edges from the cooked white.

2 Heat the olive oil in a large shallow pan. Add the shallot and cook gently for about 5 minutes until softened but not coloured, stirring occasionally. Stir in the curry powder, thyme and bay leaf and cook for 1 minute, stirring.

3 Pour the stock into a pan and bring to a gentle simmer. Stir the rice into the shallot mixture and cook for 1–2 minutes or until the rice is opaque. Add a ladleful of the simmering stock and allow it to reduce, stirring until it is completely absorbed. Continue adding the stock a ladleful at a time, stirring frequently. Allow each addition of stock to be absorbed before adding the next.

4 Meanwhile, heat the milk in a pan. Add the haddock and simmer for 1–2 minutes, depending on how thick the fillet is. Remove from the heat and leave until cool enough to handle, then remove the haddock from the poaching liquid and flake into bite-sized pieces, discarding the skin and bones.

5 Preheat the grill to hot. Arrange the pancetta or streaky bacon on the grill rack and cook for 1–2 minutes on each side until crisp and golden. Drain on kitchen paper and set aside to crisp up.

6 After about 15 minutes, add the last ladleful of stock to the rice mixture with the peas and continue to cook until the rice is just tender but still has a little bite –

al dente. Add the poached eggs to a pan of boiling salted water and just heat through for 1–2 minutes. Remove with a slotted spoon and drain on kitchen paper.

7 Add the butter to the risotto with the mascarpone and parsley, stirring energetically to combine. Fold in the flaked haddock and allow to just warm through. Add a squeeze of lemon juice and season to taste. Spoon the risotto into wide-rimmed bowls and garnish with the crispy pancetta. Place a poached egg on top of each one and serve at once.

6 Steamed Mussels with Wine, Garlic and Parsley

MITCH TONKS
STARTER

Serves 4

2 tbsp olive oil

2 shallots, finely chopped

2 garlic cloves, finely chopped

150 ml/¼ pint dry white wine, about 1 glass

500 g/1 lb 2 oz live mussels, cleaned

large handful of chopped fresh flat-leaf parsley

crusty fresh bread and aïoli, to serve

Everyone loves a bowl of steaming fragrant mussels. They should be fat, juicy and smothered in heaps of garlic and fresh parsley. Often you see cream added to the sauce but I prefer mussels plain and simple in their own juices. I enjoy them with a bowl of aïoli (garlic-flavoured mayonnaise) on the table, some good hard-crusted fresh bread and a generous supply of chilled white wine.

1 Heat a large pan with a lid. Add the olive oil and then tip in the shallots and garlic. Sauté for 3–4 minutes until softened but not coloured.

2 Pour the wine into the pan and bring to the boil, then boil fast for 2 minutes to take out some of the alcohol.

3 Add the mussels to the pan with half of the parsley and cover tightly with a lid. Cook over a high heat for 3–4 minutes, shaking the pan occasionally, until all the mussels have opened – discard any that do not.

4 Ladle the mussels into bowls with their cooking juices. Garnish with the remaining parsley and serve at once with some bread and aïoli for dunking.

7 Quick and Easy Sushi Maki

MERRILEES PARKER
STARTER

Serves 6

350 g/12 oz sushi rice

50 ml/2 fl oz mirin

5 nori sushi sheets

3 tsp wasabi paste

350 g/12 oz tuna, cut into long thin strips (sashimi quality)

5 spring onions, trimmed

1 cucumber, cut into 5 long pieces

light soy sauce and Japanese pickled ginger, to serve

Fresh sushi tastes better than bought, you can use any filling you want – you don't have to be restricted to raw fish – and it is far easier to assemble than you might imagine. Try crab and avocado with rocket or chives or a vegetarian alternative of avocado, cucumber, rocket, mint and spring onion.

1 Place the rice in a sieve and rinse very well under cold running water. Drain thoroughly and put into a large pan that has a lid. Pour over 600 ml/1 pint of water. Bring to the boil, then reduce the heat and allow to simmer for about 25 minutes or until nearly all the water has been absorbed. Remove from the heat, cover with a lid and leave to stand for 10 minutes.

2 Tip the rice on to a large, flat, clean tray – metallic is probably best as it will help the rice cool down more quickly. Dress the rice with the mirin, turning frequently (this helps the rice to cool), then wave with a fan or a magazine until the rice is at room temperature (not essential but quite authentic).

3 To make the sushi, take a bamboo sushi mat and place a sheet of the seaweed on top. Have the end you will roll from closest to you, and have a small bowl of water to hand. Dip your fingers in the water, then, taking a little rice at a time, spread it over two thirds of the seaweed, leaving the third the furthest away from you plain and pushing it to the edges to create a layer about 1 cm/½ in thick.

4 Next, smear a little wasabi in a horizontal line across the rice, a little off-centre nearest to your body. Follow with a line of tuna, a spring onion, trimmed down to fit, and a piece of cucumber. This will ensure that the filling stays in the middle of the sushi. Roll up the bamboo mat slowly, tucking in the closer end of the sushi roll to start, pressing lightly with both hands, and ending up wrapping the free bit of the seaweed around the roll. Remove from the mat and leave to sit with the joining edges downwards. You can wrap in cling film and keep in a cool place for up to 1 hour until you are ready to serve. Don't place in the fridge as this dries out the rice. Repeat until all the ingredients have been used up.

5 To serve, use a lightly moistened sharp knife to trim the ends, and then cut each roll into 6–8 pieces – you should have 30–40 pieces in total. Arrange on plates and serve with tiny bowls of the soy sauce and pickled ginger.

8 Salt and Pepper Squid with Oriental Dipping Sauce

ED BAINES
STARTER

Serves 4

vegetable oil, for deep-frying

2 egg whites

125 g/4½ oz plain flour

250 ml/9 fl oz ice-cold water

450 g/1 lb squid, cleaned

FOR THE ORIENTAL DIPPING SAUCE:

2 tbsp dark soy sauce

2 tbsp teriyaki sauce

1 tbsp clear honey

1 tbsp chopped fresh coriander

1 tsp finely grated fresh root ginger

1 garlic clove, finely chopped

juice of ½ lime

salt and freshly ground black pepper

lime wedges, to serve

This has to be one of my favourite starters – I always order it if I see it on a menu. The Japanese-style batter should be used immediately it's made, and the result should be light and crisp. The idea is to barely coat the squid so that the batter looks almost transparent when cooked. Try to get your fishmonger to skin and gut the squid for you – it can be a messy job.

1 To make the dipping sauce, place the soy sauce in a bowl and add the teriyaki sauce, honey, coriander, ginger, garlic and lime juice. Whisk until well combined. Cover with cling film and set aside until ready to use.

2 Heat a deep-fat fryer or a deep-sided pan half filled with oil to 190°C/375°F. Using a sharp knife, cut each squid tube open and then roughly chop into small pieces.

3 To make the batter, place the egg whites in a bowl with a pinch of salt and whisk with an electric mixer until stiff peaks form. Sift the flour into a bowl, make a well in the centre and gradually whisk in the iced water. Fold in the egg whites and season generously.

4 Dip a batch of the squid – depending on the size of your pan – into the batter, shaking off any excess. Using a long-pronged fork or large slotted spoon, quickly lower into the heated oil and cook for 3–4 minutes until crisp and golden brown. Remove and drain on kitchen paper. Repeat with the remaining squid.

5 Arrange the salt and pepper squid on plates with tiny bowls of the dipping sauce to the side. Garnish with lime wedges and serve at once.

9 King Prawn Caesar Salad

MIKE ROBINSON
STARTER

Serves 2

2 slices country-style bread

olive oil, for cooking

1 garlic clove, peeled and
halved

1 fresh thyme sprig

100 g/4 oz streaky bacon
lardons

4 rindless streaky bacon rashers

2 small cos or romaine lettuces,
separated into leaves and
shredded

6 large raw king prawns,
peeled and veins removed

1 lime, halved

FOR THE DRESSING:

175 g/6 oz ready-made mayonnaise

juice of 1 lemon

2 tbsp extra virgin olive oil

2 garlic cloves, crushed

2–3 canned anchovies in olive
oil, drained and finely chopped

salt and freshly ground black
pepper

This is a variation on the classic Caesar salad, the result rather like a posh prawn cocktail. It would work well as a starter or light lunch on a warm summer's day. The combination of succulent prawns with anchovy-flavoured dressing and crispy bacon works particularly well.

1 To make the dressing, place the mayonnaise in a small bowl and beat in the lemon juice, olive oil, garlic and anchovies. Season to taste, cover with cling film and chill until ready to use.

2 To make the croûtons, heat a large heavy-based frying pan. Remove the crusts from the bread and cut into 1 cm/$\frac{1}{2}$ in cubes. Add a thin film of oil to the pan and then add the bread cubes, garlic and thyme. Cook over a fairly low heat for 8–10 minutes until the croûtons are crisp and golden brown, tossing occasionally to ensure they colour evenly. Drain on kitchen paper and set aside.

3 Add another thin film of oil to the pan you made the croûtons in. Tip in the streaky bacon lardons and sauté for 3–4 minutes until crisp and golden brown. Drain on kitchen paper and set aside. Add the bacon rashers to the pan and cook for a minute or so on each side until crisp and golden brown. Drain on kitchen paper and set aside to crisp up.

4 Heat a griddle pan until smoking hot. Meanwhile, place the lettuce in a large bowl and add enough of the dressing to just coat (not drown) the leaves, then fold in the bacon lardons. Arrange on plates and scatter over the croûtons.

5 Brush the heated pan with a little oil and add the prawns. Cook for 10–20 seconds on each side until cooked through and lightly charred. Squeeze over the lime juice, season to taste and arrange on the salad. Garnish with the streaky bacon rashers and serve at once.

10 Tuna Carpaccio with Rocket and Chilli Tomato Dressing

MIKE ROBINSON
STARTER

Serves 4

2 tbsp crushed dried chilli flakes

2 tbsp coarsely ground black pepper

450 g/1 lb piece of tuna loin fillet, well trimmed

vegetable oil, for brushing

400 g/14 oz can chopped tomatoes

1 large fresh red chilli, chopped

100 g/4 oz sugar

150 g/5 oz wild rocket leaves

about 1 tbsp freshly squeezed lemon juice

about 2 tbsp extra virgin olive oil

salt and freshly ground black pepper

The idea of this starter is that the raw tuna is cooked on a searing-hot griddle pan so briefly that only the outside is coloured and caramelized and the inside is practically raw. Ask your fishmonger for sashimi-quality tuna – you won't be disappointed.

1 Heat a heavy-based griddle pan until smoking hot. Place the chilli flakes and pepper on a flat plate and mix to combine. Brush the piece of tuna with oil and roll in the chilli and pepper mixture. Add to the griddle pan and cook for 2 minutes on each side, until coloured all over. Remember the centre of the tuna should remain raw. Remove from the pan, transfer to a plate and leave in the fridge to chill for 30 minutes.

2 Meanwhile, to make the dressing, place the tomatoes and chilli in a food processor or liquidizer and whiz until blended. Pass through a fine sieve into a bowl. Put the sugar in a small heavy-based pan with 100 ml/3½ fl oz of water. Bring to the boil, stirring until the sugar has completely dissolved, and then tip in the tomato and chilli mixture. Reduce the heat and simmer gently for 8–10 minutes or until the dressing has reduced to a syrup-like consistency, stirring occasionally. Season to taste and leave to cool completely.

3 Place the rocket in a bowl and season to taste, then dress with enough lemon juice and olive oil just to coat the leaves. Pile up in the centre of cold plates. Slice the tuna into 0.5 cm/¼ in slices and arrange around the rocket. Dribble over the chilli tomato dressing and serve at once.

11 Goats' Cheese Parcels

MIKE ROBINSON
STARTER

Serves 2

75 g/3 oz goats' Cheddar, cut into 1 cm/¹/₂ in cubes

1 tsp chopped fresh thyme

1 tsp chopped fresh marjoram

1 garlic clove, finely chopped

about 2 tsp olive oil

40 g/1¹/₂ oz unsalted butter

2 large filo pastry sheets, thawed if frozen

salt and freshly ground black pepper

strawberry confiture, to serve (optional)

This very simple starter is a masterpiece – everyone will think you've been slaving away in the kitchen for hours. Choose the type of goats' cheese you use carefully as its flavour will determine the success of the dish. I like to serve the parcels with a spoonful of a good-quality shop-bought strawberry confiture (that's jam!).

1 Preheat the oven to 200°C/400°F/Gas Mark 6 (fan oven 180°C from cold). Place the goats' cheese Cheddar in a bowl with the thyme, marjoram and garlic. Add enough olive oil just to bind the mixture together. Season to taste.

2 Melt the butter in a small pan or in the microwave. Leave to cool a little. Brush each sheet of filo pastry on both sides with most of the melted butter. Lay the buttered sheets of filo on top of each other and cut in half, then cut each half into three to make six even-sized rectangles.

3 Divide the cheese mixture among the filo rectangles, placing a small mound in the centre of each one. Carefully roll up into a spring roll shape to enclose and twist both ends like a cracker. Put on a non-stick baking sheet a little way apart. Brush with the remaining butter and bake for about 4 minutes or until the pastry is crisp and golden brown. Arrange on plates with a spoonful of confiture to the side, if using. Serve at once.

12 Parma Ham-wrapped Asparagus with Tapenade

ANTONY WORRALL
THOMPSON
STARTER

Serves 4

20 small asparagus spears, trimmed

20 slices Parma ham

FOR THE TAPENADE:

450 g/1 lb pitted black olives, marinated in olive oil and drained

75 g/3 oz capers, drained and rinsed

12 fresh basil leaves, ripped

1 tbsp aged red wine vinegar

2 tsp Dijon mustard

175 ml/6 fl oz extra virgin olive oil

3 tbsp chopped fresh flat-leaf parsley (optional)

salt and freshly ground black pepper

British asparagus is hailed by leading chefs as the best in the world: the climate allows the asparagus stems to develop slowly, producing a full, sweet flavour and a fine, tender texture quite unlike any other crop. Unfortunately, it's only in season for roughly eight weeks in May and June, so buy it while you can. This recipe uses small, tender specimens to create simple and delicious finger food. The tapenade makes about 675 g/1½ lb in total but it will keep happily in the fridge for a couple of weeks.

1 To make the tapenade, place the olives, capers and basil in a food processor or liquidizer. Add the vinegar, mustard and olive oil, and a teaspoon of ground black pepper. Blend until smoothish, allowing some texture to remain. Fold in parsley, if using, and season with salt to taste. Transfer to a bowl and cover with cling film, or use a sterilised Kilner jar. Chill until ready to use.

2 Cook the asparagus spears for 3–6 minutes, depending on their size, in a large pan of boiling water or in a steamer standing in 7.5 cm/3 in of boiling water until just tender. Drain and quickly refresh in a bowl of ice-cold water, then set aside until completely cool.

3 Spread each slice of Parma ham thinly with some of the tapenade and then use to wrap each cooked asparagus spear. Arrange on plates or one large platter to serve.

13 Bruschetta with Chicken Livers in Red Wine Sauce

MIKE ROBINSON
STARTER

Serves 2

8 fresh chicken livers (or thawed if frozen)

150 ml/¼ pint milk

1 garlic clove, peeled

4 slices sourdough bread

40 g/1½ oz seasoned flour

25 g/1 oz unsalted butter

2 shallots, finely chopped

½ tsp fresh thyme leaves

about 50 ml/2 fl oz red wine

2 tbsp beef stock (from a carton is fine)

1 tsp balsamic vinegar

½ tsp tomato purée

salt and freshly ground black pepper

This topping is classic French peasant food at its best, and the bruschetta uses up any stale bread that's left over in the kitchen. Chicken livers are good value for money and don't get used often enough in my opinion. Try to find free-range or organic: the flavour is always much better. You need to soak the chicken livers overnight for this recipe.

1 Trim the chicken livers well and place in a non-metallic bowl. Pour over the milk and cover with cling film. Place in the fridge overnight to soak.

2 Preheat the grill. Cut the garlic clove in half and rub all over the bread, then finely chop the garlic and set aside to use later. Arrange the bread on a grill rack and lightly toast on both sides. Keep warm.

3 Meanwhile, heat a heavy-based frying pan for the chicken livers. Drain the livers from the milk, shaking off any excess, and then coat in a light dusting of the seasoned flour. Add the butter to the pan and, once it has stopped foaming, add the chicken livers. Seal for 1 minute on each side until golden brown but not cooked through.

4 Tip the shallots into the pan of chicken livers with the reserved garlic and the thyme, tossing until well coated. Continue to cook for another minute or so until the shallots have begun to soften.

5 Deglaze the pan with a good splash of red wine, scraping the bottom with a wooden spoon to remove any sediment. Add the stock, balsamic vinegar and tomato purée and simmer to reduce a little, stirring constantly. Season to taste. Arrange the toasted bread on plates and spoon the chicken livers in red wine sauce on top to serve.

14 Fig and Pancetta Tart with Dolcelatte and Herb Salad

JAMES MARTIN
STARTER

Serves 4

100 g/4 oz ready-made puff pastry, thawed if frozen

a little plain flour, for dusting

knob of unsalted butter, for greasing

8 large ripe figs

150 g/5 oz dolcelatte cheese, diced

6 thin slices pancetta

2–3 tbsp extra virgin olive oil

a little beaten egg, for glazing

100 ml/3½ fl oz double cream

FOR THE SALAD:

small bunch of fresh coriander, leaves stripped

small bunch of fresh mint, leaves stripped

100 g/4 oz tender young spinach

1 tsp balsamic vinegar

salt and freshly ground black pepper

This luscious summer tart would make a fantastic Sunday lunch on a hot summer's day. The combination of warm figs and salty melted dolcelatte is sublime and needs nothing more than the herb salad to serve. I always use ready-made puff pastry, as do most chefs, if they're honest. It saves so much messing around (and for me it keeps a nagging pastry chef out of the kitchen!).

1 Roll out the pastry on a lightly floured board to a round or square that is about 25 cm/10 in diameter. Place on a buttered baking sheet, then chill in the fridge for at least 30 minutes.

2 Meanwhile, preheat the oven to 200°C/400°F/Gas Mark 6 (fan oven 180°C from cold). Cut the figs into quarters. Remove the baking sheet from the fridge and arrange the figs over the pastry, leaving a 1 cm/½ in gap around the edge.

3 Dot the dolcelatte over the figs and arrange the pancetta on top. Season to taste and drizzle over a tablespoon of the olive oil. Brush the edges of the tart with the beaten egg and bake for 10 minutes.

4 Remove the tart from the oven and carefully pour over the cream. Sprinkle a few of the coriander leaves on top and bake for another 6–8 minutes until the pastry is cooked through, puffed up and golden.

5 Meanwhile, make the salad. Place the remaining coriander leaves in a bowl with the mint and baby spinach. Dress with a little olive oil and the balsamic vinegar. Season to taste. Transfer the cooked tart to a large plate and serve warm with a bowl of the salad so that everyone can help themselves.

15 Thai Chicken Patties with a Sweet Chilli Dipping Sauce

MIKE ROBINSON
STARTER

Serves 2

200 g/7 oz minced chicken

25 g/1 oz bunch of fresh coriander, finely chopped (stalks and leaves)

1 red chilli, seeded and finely chopped

2 garlic cloves, finely chopped

1 lemongrass stalk, outer leaves removed and remainder finely chopped

5 cm/2 in piece of fresh root ginger, peeled and finely chopped

1 tbsp dark soy sauce

2 kaffir lime leaves, finely shredded

juice of 1 lime

about 2 tbsp vegetable oil

about 2 tbsp sesame oil

6 spring onions, trimmed

FOR THE CHILLI SAUCE:

100 g/4 oz caster sugar

25 g/1 oz dried chilli flakes

salt and freshly ground black pepper

chopped fresh coriander, to garnish

The lemongrass, lime leaves and masses of coriander make these morsels fragrant. Lean minced chicken is very low in fat and now widely available. To make the patties even healthier, instead of frying them try brushing them with a little oil and then baking them in a preheated oven at 200°C/400°F/Gas Mark 6 (fan oven 180°C from cold) for 8–10 minutes, turning halfway through, until golden brown.

1 To make the chilli sauce, place the sugar in a small heavy-based pan with 100 ml/3½ fl oz water and bring to the boil, stirring until the sugar has completely dissolved. Add the chilli flakes, reduce the heat and simmer gently for about 40 minutes until reduced to a syrup-like consistency. Remove from the heat and leave to cool.

2 To make the chicken patties, place the minced chicken in a bowl with the coriander, chilli, garlic, lemongrass, ginger, soy sauce, kaffir lime leaves and lime juice. Season and mix until well combined. Cover with cling film and chill for 20 minutes to allow the flavours to combine.

3 Heat a large frying pan. Using slightly wetted hands, shape the chicken mixture into small patties, each about the size of a tablespoon. Add the vegetable oil to the pan with half of the sesame oil and then add the chicken patties. Cook for 5 minutes on each side until cooked through and golden brown – you may have to do this in batches depending on the size of your pan. Drain on kitchen paper.

4 Meanwhile, heat a griddle pan until smoking hot. Brush the spring onions with the remaining sesame oil and griddle for 2 minutes until heated through and lightly charred, turning occasionally. Arrange on plates and place the chicken patties on top, then garnish with the coriander. Divide the chilli sauce among small dipping bowls and place one on each plate to serve.

16 Crispy Fried Goats' Cheese Salad

PAUL RANKIN
SNACKS & LIGHT BITES

Serves 4

300 g/11 oz goats' cheese log

1 egg

2 tbsp milk

a little plain flour, for dredging

100 g/4 oz fresh white bread-crumbs

vegetable oil, for frying

1 small, firm, ripe avocado

100 g/4 oz mixed salad leaves

50 g/2 oz walnuts, lightly toasted and skinned

20 small black olives

FOR THE DRESSING:

4 tbsp extra virgin olive oil

4 tbsp walnut or hazelnut oil

2 tbsp red wine vinegar

1 tsp Dijon mustard

salt and freshly ground black pepper

fresh chervil sprigs, to garnish

I first tried this kind of salad in San Francisco at Chez Panisse – it was made popular by US restaurants like this, and chefs like me brought it back to the UK. Now it is a firm favourite in our household, as well as at the restaurant. There's just something so appealing about a good fresh goats' cheese encased in a crisp crumb. For an option that's lower in calories, omit the breadcrumb stage, and melt the goats' cheese under the grill instead.

1 Allow the goats' cheese to come to room temperature. Dip a knife in hot water and slice the log into four even-sized pieces. Break the egg into a shallow dish and beat with the milk. Dredge each goats' cheese slice in flour, and then dip into the egg mixture and finally in the breadcrumbs, pressing them in firmly to cover each piece.

2 To make the dressing, place the olive oil in a small bowl with the walnut or hazelnut oil, vinegar and mustard. Whisk together until well combined and season to taste.

3 Heat a frying pan over medium heat. Pour in enough vegetable oil to coat the bottom of the pan by 0.5 cm/¼ in. When the oil is hot, carefully add the coated goat's cheese slices and cook them for about 2 minutes on each side until crisp and golden brown. Remove from the pan and drain on kitchen paper.

4 Meanwhile, cut the avocado in half and remove the stone, then scoop out the flesh and cut into dice. Place in a large bowl with the salad leaves, walnuts and olives. Drizzle over half of the dressing and toss lightly to coat. Arrange a mound of the salad mixture in the centre of each plate, and top with the crispy goats' cheese. Spoon around the remaining dressing and garnish with chervil sprigs to serve.

17 Hot Smoked Salmon with Warm Potato and Mangetout Salad

MIKE ROBINSON
SNACKS & LIGHT BITES

Serves 2

1 tbsp maple syrup

**1 tbsp *ketjap manis*
(Indonesian sweet soy sauce)**

juice of 1 lime

1 shallot, finely chopped

1 garlic clove, finely chopped

**knob of fresh root ginger,
peeled and finely chopped**

**2 x 150 g/5 oz salmon fillets,
skinned**

300 g/11 oz baby new potatoes

knob of unsalted butter

1 tbsp extra virgin olive oil

**1 tsp freshly squeezed lemon
juice**

**150 g/5 oz mangetout,
trimmed**

**handful of shredded fresh basil
and coriander**

**salt and freshly ground black
pepper**

You'll need a large roll of tin foil and some smoked oakwood chippings for this. Here the dish is made in a griddle pan but it could also be cooked on the barbecue or in a hot oven. *Ketjap manis* is now available in large supermarkets – it is much thicker than Chinese and Japanese soy sauces, almost syrup-like, with a sweeter, more intense flavour. I use it all the time in marinades or just as a condiment, and love its unique flavour.

1 Place the maple syrup in a small bowl and stir in the *ketjap manis*, lime juice, shallot, garlic and ginger until well combined. Take a 30 cm/12 in square sheet of foil and arrange the two salmon fillets side by side on one half. Drizzle over the maple syrup mixture and season to taste. Fold the foil sheet over to enclose the salmon fillets completely and secure tightly into an envelope shape.

2 Take another 30 cm/12 in square sheet of foil and sprinkle the smoked oakwood chippings on one half. Place the foil parcel containing the salmon fillets on top and prick the parcel about 20 times with the tip of a sharp knife. Fold the bottom sheet of foil over to enclose the salmon parcel and secure into an envelope shape.

3 Heat a griddle pan until smoking hot. Place the potatoes in a pan of boiling salted water, cover and simmer for 10–12 minutes until tender. Add the foil parcel to the heated griddle pan and cook for 8–10 minutes until the salmon is cooked through and tender. Drain the potatoes and place in a large bowl; add the butter, olive oil and lemon juice and gently fold with a large spoon until well combined.

4 Meanwhile, cook the mangetout in a pan of boiling salted water for 1–2 minutes until just tender but still crisp. Drain and quickly refresh under cold running water. Stir the herbs into the potatoes and arrange on plates. Scatter over the mangetout and then open the salmon parcel and place a salmon fillet on each plate. Drizzle over any remaining cooking juices from the parcel and serve at once.

18 Neapolitan-style Pizza

GENNARO CONTALDO
SNACKS & LIGHT BITES

Makes 2 large pizzas

500 g/1 lb 2 oz Italian 00 flour or strong plain flour, plus extra for dusting

10 g/¼ oz fresh yeast

325 ml/11 fl oz lukewarm water

300 g/11 oz canned plum tomatoes, well drained

4 tbsp extra virgin olive oil, plus extra for drizzling

a few dried white breadcrumbs or a little semolina

25 g/1 oz freshly grated Parmesan

few fresh basil leaves or pinch of dried oregano

150 g/5 oz mozzarella cheese, roughly chopped

salt and freshly ground black pepper

I was once lucky enough to spend time at the Pizza Academy in Naples, where they are strict about how the pizza dough is made and what toppings can be used. This is my recipe for the original Neapolitan pizza, which started off as a means of using up the housewife's leftovers: bread dough, tomatoes, cheese and whatever else was in the cupboard.

1 Place the flour in a bowl with two teaspoons of salt. Dissolve the yeast in the lukewarm water and gradually add to the flour, mixing well until you obtain a soft dough. If you find the dough too sticky, just add a little more flour. Shape the dough into a ball and leave to rest, covered with a clean tea towel, for 5 minutes. Knead the dough for 8–10 minutes, until smooth and elastic, then split in half. Knead each piece for a couple of minutes and then shape into a ball. Sprinkle a little flour on a clean tea towel and place the dough on it, then cover with a slightly damp cloth. Leave to rise for 30 minutes.

2 Meanwhile, preheat the oven to 250°C/500°F/Gas Mark 10 (fan oven 230°C from cold) – if your oven doesn't go this high, just heat it to its highest setting and cook the pizzas for a few minutes longer if necessary. Place the tomatoes in a bowl, crush them slightly with a fork, add the four tablespoons of olive oil and season to taste. Stir well to combine.

3 Sprinkle some flour on a clean work surface and with your fingers spread one piece of dough into a circle about 35–40 cm/14–16 in in diameter. Make the dough as thin as a pancake but be careful not to tear it, and make the border slightly thicker. Repeat with the other ball of dough, then sprinkle some bread-crumbs or semolina over two large, flat baking sheets and place the pizza bases on them.

4 Spread the tomatoes evenly over each base – not too much, or the pizzas will be soggy. Drizzle with olive oil, sprinkle over the Parmesan, add a few basil leaves or some oregano and top with the mozzarella. Bake for 7 minutes, or a couple of minutes longer if you prefer your pizza crisp. Remove from the oven and drizzle with a little more olive oil. Transfer to plates and eat immediately.

19 Baby Bruschettas with Poached Pears, Gorgonzola and Port Syrup

MERRILEES PARKER
SNACKS & LIGHT BITES

Serves 4–6

2 small, firm pears

2 tbsp clear honey

150 ml/¼ pint ruby red port

150 ml/¼ pint red wine

1 long thin baguette, cut into 24 slices (ends discarded)

about 2 tbsp extra virgin olive oil

225 g/8 oz Gorgonzola, at room temperature

It is important that the pears for this recipe are firm, or they will fall apart when you poach them. I like to poach them the night before as this enhances the flavour and makes them easier to handle. It also allows the syrup to cool and thicken. If you come to use the syrup and it is too thick, add a little warm water. If it is too thin you can reduce it for a minute or two longer.

1 Preheat the grill to hot. Halve and core the pears, then cut each half into 6 small wedges. Place in a heavy-based pan with the honey, port and wine. Cook for 10–15 minutes or until the pears are tender when pierced with the point of a sharp knife but not at all soft.

2 Drain the liquid into a small pan and set the pear wedges aside to drain thoroughly. Simmer the liquid for 8–10 minutes until reduced by two-thirds to a syrupy consistency that will coat the back of a spoon. Place in a small bowl and leave to cool.

3 To make the bruschettas, brush each slice of bread with a little of the olive oil and arrange on a grill rack. Grill for 1–2 minutes until toasted and golden, turning once.

4 To serve, generously spread each bruschetta with Gorgonzola and top with a poached pear slice. Finally, using a teaspoon, drizzle over the port syrup. Arrange on a large platter or plates to serve.

32

20 Hot Artichoke 'Sin' with Tortilla Chips

CELIA BROOKS BROWN
SNACKS & LIGHT BITES

Serves 2

400 g/14 oz can artichoke hearts, well drained and roughly chopped

250 ml/9 fl oz ready-made mayonnaise

150 g/5 oz freshly grated Parmesan

2 green chillies, seeded and finely chopped

200 g/7 oz packet plain tortilla chips

salt and freshly ground black pepper

This is a traditional American dip which I call 'sin' because it's the most wicked, naughty and indulgent treat I know … I bake it in a round terracotta baking dish so it can be taken from the oven straight to the table.

1 Preheat the oven to 220°C/425°F/Gas Mark 7 (fan oven 200°C from cold). Place the artichokes in a bowl and mix in the mayonnaise, Parmesan and chillies. Season to taste and spoon into a baking dish in a layer that is no more than 2 cm/¾ in deep. Bake for about 15 minutes until bubbling and golden. Place the dish on a large heatproof platter and pile around the tortilla chips for scooping. Serve at once.

21 Spanish-Style Baked Eggs

CURTIS STONE
SNACKS & LIGHT BITES

Serves 1

3 tbsp olive oil

2 shallots, finely chopped

1 garlic clove, crushed

1 mild red chilli, seeded and finely chopped

1 small uncooked chorizo, peeled and sliced (optional)

10 salted capers, soaked in water for 30 minutes and drained

2 tsp sherry or red wine vinegar

400 g/14 oz can chopped tomatoes

2 tsp chopped fresh flat-leaf parsley

2 large eggs

salt and freshly ground black pepper

fresh chervil sprigs, to garnish

crusty bread, to serve

This recipe doesn't take much preparation. It has come to the rescue on many an occasion when I've found myself with very little in the fridge and too tired to make it to the shops after a long shift at the restaurant. Serve it immediately with chunks of rustic bread to mop up all the delicious juices.

1 Preheat the oven to 160°C/325°F/Gas Mark 3 (fan oven 140°C from cold). Heat the olive oil in a large frying or sauté pan. Add the shallots, garlic, chilli and chorizo, if using, and sauté for 2–3 minutes until the shallots are softened and the chorizo is just beginning to sizzle.

2 Stir the capers into the pan with the vinegar and simmer for 1 minute. Add the chopped tomatoes and parsley and bring to the boil, stirring. Remove from the heat and season to taste.

3 Transfer the tomato sauce to a small ovenproof dish. Make two slight indentations and gently break in the eggs. Season the eggs and then cover the dish with foil. Bake for 8–10 minutes until the eggs have set but the yolks are still runny; cook for a minute or two longer if you like your eggs more well done. Garnish with chervil and serve at once with some crusty bread.

22 Penne with Pancetta and Sun-dried Tomatoes

GINO D'ACAMPO
SNACKS & LIGHT BITES

Serves 2

225 g/8 oz penne pasta (good quality)

3 tbsp extra virgin olive oil

1 onion, finely sliced

150 g/5 oz pancetta lardons (Italian streaky bacon)

75 g/3 oz frozen peas, thawed

4–6 sun-dried tomatoes in oil, sliced

salt

chilli-flavoured olive oil, to garnish

This recipe comes from my home town, Torre Del Greco, very near Naples. Every restaurant there has its own version but this is the one I grew up with. For me, peas and pancetta are the ultimate combination, the sweetness of the peas complementing the smokiness of the pancetta.

1 Plunge the pasta into a large pan of boiling salted water, stir once and simmer for 8–10 minutes or according to packet instructions until al dente, tender to the bite.

2 Meanwhile, heat a large frying pan. Add the olive oil and sauté the onion until softened but not coloured. Add the pancetta and continue to cook for another few minutes until the pancetta is crisp and golden.

3 Stir the peas and sun-dried tomatoes into the onion and pancetta mixture and cook for another minute or two until heated through, stirring occasionally. Season with a pinch of salt.

4 Drain the pasta and return to the pan. Tip in the sauce and toss until well combined. Divide among wide-rimmed bowls and drizzle over the chilli oil. Serve at once.

23 Crispy Tuna Fingers with Tomato, Courgette and Olive Compote

ED BAINES
SNACKS & LIGHT BITES

Serves 2

100 g/4 oz fresh white breadcrumbs

1 tsp dried oregano

grated rind of 1 lime

2 eggs

100 ml/3½ fl oz milk

100 g/4 oz seasoned flour

225 g/8 oz tuna steak

4 tbsp vegetable oil

FOR THE COMPOTE:

75 ml/3 fl oz olive oil

1 small red onion, chopped

1 garlic clove, finely chopped

225 g/8 oz courgettes, diced

4 ripe tomatoes, peeled and roughly chopped

25 g/1 oz pitted green and black olives, chopped

1 canned anchovy fillet, finely chopped

1 tsp white wine vinegar

4 tbsp torn fresh basil

juice of 1 lime

salt and freshly ground black pepper

This is my twist on the humble fishfinger. The tuna is cut into finger-sized pieces, coated in breadcrumbs and then shallow-fried. The secret is to cook the tuna fingers over a fairly high heat to seal the outside and create a crisp exterior, while the tuna inside remains moist and tender. They make a perfect snack and are universally popular with adults and children alike.

1 To make the compote, heat the olive oil in a large pan and sauté the onion and garlic until softened but not coloured. Increase the heat and add the courgettes. Continue to cook for 2 minutes until well coated and just beginning to soften.

2 Add the tomatoes to the pan with the olives, anchovy, vinegar, basil, lime juice and seasoning. Stir until well combined, then reduce the heat to its lowest setting and simmer gently for 10–15 minutes until well reduced and thickened, stirring occasionally.

3 Meanwhile, make the crispy tuna fingers. Place the breadcrumbs, oregano and lime rind in a shallow dish, season to taste and mix to combine. Place the eggs and milk in a separate shallow dish. Season generously and whisk until well combined. Place the flour on a flat plate.

4 Cut the tuna into fingers, about 7.5 cm/3 in x 2 cm/¾ in, and toss to coat in the flour, shaking off any excess. Dip into the egg mixture and then cover with the breadcrumbs.

5 Heat the vegetable oil in a large frying pan over a moderate heat. Add the coated tuna fingers and cook for a minute or two on each side until crisp and golden brown. Drain well on kitchen paper. Arrange stacks of the crispy tuna fingers on plates and add a large spoonful of the compote to serve.

24 Honey and Mustard-glazed Chicken Salad with Pine Nuts and Goats' Cheese

JAMES TANNER
SNACKS & LIGHT BITES

Serves 2

50 g/2 oz pine nuts

2 tbsp extra virgin olive oil

1 tbsp balsamic vinegar

**2 tbsp clear honey, plus
1 teaspoon**

2 tsp wholegrain mustard

**1 large skinless chicken breast
fillet, cut into strips**

olive oil, for brushing

50 g/2 oz rocket leaves

**100 g/4 oz goats' cheese (such
as crottin)**

**salt and freshly ground black
pepper**

Glazed chicken strips on a mound of lightly dressed rocket leaves – a perfect lunch or light supper. The chicken can be left to marinate up to 24 hours in advance and kept covered with cling film in the fridge until ready to cook.

1 Heat a heavy-based frying pan. Add the pine nuts and dry-fry for about 5 minutes until toasted, tossing occasionally to ensure they colour evenly. Tip on to a plate and leave to cool completely.

2 To make the dressing, place the extra virgin olive oil in a bowl with the balsamic vinegar and season to taste. Whisk until well combined.

3 Heat a heavy-based griddle pan. Place the two tablespoons of honey in a bowl and whisk in the mustard. Add the chicken and turn to coat. Brush the heated griddle pan with a little olive oil and add the chicken strips. Cook for 2–3 minutes on each side or until cooked through and lightly charred.

4 Place the rocket leaves in a bowl and add enough of the dressing to barely coat the leaves. Arrange small, high mounds on each plate. Stack the chicken strips on top and crumble over the goats' cheese. Scatter over the pine nuts and drizzle the remaining teaspoon of honey around the edges of the plates to serve.

25 Korean Beef in Lettuce

JILL DUPLEIX
SNACKS & LIGHT BITES

Serves 4

2 sirloin steaks, each about
2.5 cm/1 in thick

1 round soft-leaved lettuce,
such as oak leaf or mignonette

300 g/11 oz Thai fragrant rice,
well rinsed

2 tbsp dark soy sauce

2 tbsp chilli bean sauce or
sweet chilli sauce

1 tbsp toasted sesame seeds

FOR THE MARINADE:

2 spring onions, finely chopped

2 garlic cloves, crushed

5 cm/2 in piece of fresh root
ginger, peeled and grated

1 tbsp toasted sesame oil

2 tbsp Shaoxing rice wine or
dry sherry

3 tbsp dark soy sauce

1 tbsp chilli bean sauce or
sweet chilli sauce

$\frac{1}{2}$ tsp freshly ground black
pepper

1 tbsp caster sugar

This is inspired by the traditional Korean way of cooking called *bulgogi*, where the meat is cooked on a hot stone or griddle at the table and served with lots of fresh, clean flavours. The slightly smoky flavours of beef seared at high temperatures go well with the blandness of the rice and the crunchiness of the lettuce. Try not to overcook the steak. It should be served pink in the middle. Allow your guests to assemble the lettuce leaves themselves, and have fun.

1 To make the marinade, place the spring onions in a shallow non-metallic dish with the garlic, ginger, sesame oil, rice wine or sherry, soy, chilli bean or sweet chilli sauce, pepper and sugar, whisking until well combined. Thinly slice the sirloin steaks, against the grain, and add to the marinade, turning until well coated. Cover with cling film and chill for at least 1 hour (or overnight is fine).

2 Remove the outer leaves from the lettuce and discard, then gently remove the remainder and wash under cold running water. Drain well on kitchen paper and place in a bowl. Cover loosely with cling film and chill until ready to use.

3 Put the rice in a heavy-based saucepan with 600 ml/1 pint cold water, bring to the boil and jam the lid on tight. Simmer over the lowest possible heat for 16 minutes, then leave, covered and off the heat, for 5 minutes. To make the soy chilli sauce, place the soy sauce in a small bowl and stir in the chilli sauce.

4 Heat a heavy-based non-stick frying pan until hot. Sear the beef for 1–2 minutes until lightly browned but still pink in the middle. Transfer to a warm serving platter – you may have to do this in batches, depending on the size of your pan. Sprinkle over the sesame seeds.

5 To serve, fluff up the rice with a fork, then place the platter of beef straight on the table with the hot rice, lettuce leaves and soy chilli sauce. Allow each person to help themselves: by spooning a little of the rice on to a lettuce leaf, adding a slice or two of the beef and a little of the soy chilli sauce, then rolling it up to eat.

26 Squid with Chorizo and Beans

JILL DUPLEIX
FISH & SHELLFISH

Serves 4

1 tbsp olive oil

4 fresh chorizo sausages, thickly sliced on the diagonal

2 x 400 g/14 oz cans cannellini beans, drained and well rinsed

2 tsp smoked paprika

100 ml/3½ fl oz fresh chicken stock

450 g/1 lb squid, cleaned

150 g/5 oz plain flour

3 tbsp olive oil, plus a little extra if needed

100 g/4 oz rocket leaves

salt and freshly ground black pepper

lemon wedges, to serve

Buy spanking fresh squid from your fishmonger for this dish and make sure you get him to clean it for you. This bean stew is a great winter warmer that packs a subtle, smoky, chorizo punch. Use any variety of white bean – or swap the beans for tinned chickpeas – and look for chorizo that is suitable for cooking, normally similar in size to the British breakfast pork sausage.

1 Heat the olive oil in a large frying pan. Add the chorizo and fry for a few minutes until the slices have begun to crisp around the edges. Add the beans, then stir in half of the paprika and pour in the stock. Bring the boil, then reduce the heat and simmer gently for 5 minutes until almost all the stock has evaporated, stirring occasionally. Season to taste.

2 Cut the bodies of the squid into 1 cm/½ in rings and cut the tentacles into small sections. Place the flour in a bowl and add the remaining paprika, a teaspoon of salt and half a teaspoon of pepper, stirring to combine. Place a colander in the sink. Toss a handful of the squid into the seasoned flour, then tip into the colander and shake vigorously to get rid of any excess.

3 Heat a large, non-stick frying pan for the squid. Add the extra virgin olive oil and swirl around until hot. Scatter in a batch of the coated squid and fry very quickly, turning once with tongs. Drain on kitchen paper and repeat with the remaining ingredients, adding a little more oil, if necessary. Spoon the chorizo and beans on to plates and scatter with the rocket leaves. Arrange the fried squid on top and garnish with lemon wedges to serve.

27 Steamed Cantonese-style Fish

KEN HOM
FISH & SHELLFISH

Serves 4

450 g/1 lb firm white fish fillets, skinned, such as cod or sole

1 tsp coarse sea salt

2 cm/¾ in piece of fresh root ginger, peeled and shredded

3 spring onions, finely shredded

2 tbsp light soy sauce

2 tbsp dark soy sauce

1 tbsp groundnut oil

2 tsp toasted sesame oil

fresh coriander sprigs, to garnish

plain boiled rice, to serve (optional)

Steaming is a favourite Chinese method for cooking fish: a simple but gentle technique that doesn't mask the fresh taste of the fish and allows it to remain moist and tender. It also has the added bonus that it is very healthy. I like to use a whole fish such as Dover sole or turbot for a special occasion, but any firm white fish fillets work well.

1 Pat the fish fillets dry with kitchen paper and sprinkle all over with the salt, rubbing it in with your hands. Place on a heatproof plate and scatter the ginger on top.

2 Set up a steamer or put a rack into a wok or deep-sided pan with a lid. Pour in enough water to come 5 cm/2 in up the sides and bring to the boil.

3 Place the plate of fish on the rack, cover tightly and steam for about 5 minutes until the fish has turned opaque and is flaking slightly but is still moist.

4 Remove the plate of cooked fish and carefully drain off any liquid that has accumulated. Scatter over the spring onions and then drizzle over the light and dark soy sauces.

5 Place the groundnut and sesame oil in a small pan and heat until smoking, then immediately pour over the fish. Garnish with coriander and serve at once straight on to the table, with a separate bowl of plain boiled rice, if liked.

28 Paella

PAUL MERRETT
FISH & SHELLFISH

Serves 2

2 tbsp olive oil

2 skinless chicken breast fillets, each cut into 8 pieces

4 whole raw king prawns

20 mussels, cleaned

1 garlic clove, finely chopped

3 ripe tomatoes, peeled, seeded and chopped

200 g/7 oz Spanish short-grain rice (calasparra or paella)

pinch of saffron strands, soaked in a little warm water

1 litre/1¾ pints hot chicken stock

8 small cherry tomatoes

100 g/4 oz broad beans (fresh or frozen)

salt and freshly ground black pepper

lightly dressed rocket salad and crusty bread, to serve

This is a great one-'pot' classic Spanish dish that originated in Valencia, although there are numerous versions throughout Spain. As a rule, the nearer the coast you are the more seafood you tend to find in paella, and the further inland you go the more meat, such as rabbit and chicken, is featured. Traditionally paella is cooked in a shallow cast-iron pan over an outdoor boxwood fire. The pans are generally very cheap in Spain so why not pick one up next time you're on holiday?

1 Heat the olive oil in a paella pan or large, heavy-based sauté pan. Add the chicken and sauté for 1–2 minutes until sealed and lightly golden.

2 Add the prawns to the pan, stirring to combine, and then tip in the mussels, again stirring to combine. Add the garlic and tomatoes and sauté for another few minutes until well combined.

3 Sprinkle the rice into the pan and continue to cook for a minute or so; shake the pan occasionally but do not be tempted to stir. Add the saffron mixture and pour in the stock to the level of the rice – ensure that the ingredients in the pan are covered with stock but no more.

4 Scatter over the cherry tomatoes with the broad beans and season to taste. Bring to the boil, then reduce the heat and simmer gently for 20 minutes or until the rice is completely tender and all the liquid has been absorbed. Serve the paella pan straight on to the table with a bowl of rocket salad and a basket of crusty bread.

29 Penne with Prawns, Tomato and Crème Fraîche

ED BAINES
FISH & SHELLFISH

Serves 4

3 tbsp olive oil

1 onion, finely chopped

1 celery stick, finely chopped

1 carrot, finely chopped

1 garlic clove, finely chopped

350 g/12 oz penne pasta (good quality)

1 tbsp plain flour

1 tbsp tomato purée

juice of 1 lemon

1 bay leaf

75 ml/3 fl oz dry white wine

300 ml/½ pint fresh fish stock (from a carton is fine)

250 g/9 oz cooked peeled prawns

3 tbsp crème fraîche

4 tbsp freshly grated Parmesan

4 tbsp torn fresh basil, plus extra to garnish

salt and freshly ground black pepper

I first had this while on holiday in Italy and just loved it. It's the perfect quick supper dish, great with a glass of chilled dry white wine. Try to find our own native prawns, which are a little on the small side but do have the most delightful delicate flavour. Otherwise, splash out on the meatiest prawns that you can find for this dish; it's well worth it.

1 Heat two tablespoons of the olive oil in a large sauté pan. Add the onion, celery, carrot and garlic and cook over a low heat for 8–10 minutes until softened but not coloured, stirring occasionally.

2 Plunge the penne into a pan of boiling salted water and cook for 8–10 minutes or according to packet instructions until al dente, tender to the bite. Drain, refresh briefly under cold running water and toss in the remaining tablespoon of olive oil.

3 Sprinkle the flour over the vegetable mixture and stir in to combine. Cook for 1 minute, stirring continuously, and then stir in the tomato purée, lemon juice and bay leaf. Pour in the wine and allow to bubble down until almost evaporated, stirring occasionally.

4 Pour the fish stock into the vegetable mixture and bring to the boil, then reduce the heat and simmer until the sauce has reduced by half. Pass through a fine sieve into a clean pan and return to a simmer. Add the prawns and then stir in the crème fraîche until well combined and heated through. Season to taste.

5 Stir the cooked penne into the sauce with half of the Parmesan and the basil. Divide among wide-rimmed bowls and scatter over the remaining Parmesan. Garnish with basil and serve at once.

30 Pepper-Crusted Monkfish with Mustard Dill Sauce

JAMES MARTIN
FISH & SHELLFISH

Serves 4

550 g/1¼ lb floury potatoes, cut into chunks

100 g/4 oz green cabbage leaves, shredded

olive oil for frying

3 rindless smoky bacon rashers, chopped

1 shallot, finely chopped

2 garlic cloves, crushed

3 tbsp chopped fresh mixed herbs, such as parsley, dill and coriander

500 g/1 lb 2 oz whole monk-fish tail, filleted and skinned

3 tbsp coarsely ground black pepper

50 g/2 oz seasoned flour

FOR THE MUSTARD DILL SAUCE:

1 tbsp olive oil

1 shallot, finely chopped

1 garlic clove, finely chopped

3 tbsp white wine

100 ml/3½ fl oz double cream

3 tbsp wholegrain mustard, preferably Pomery or Gordons

2 tbsp chopped fresh dill

continued opposite

This dish has always been very popular in my restaurants. It is definitely a recipe for the more adventurous, and those of you willing to spend a little more money. The finished result will look and taste great, but is genuinely not too difficult to achieve if you follow the method below. The monkfish medallions can be prepared in advance, ready to cook, as can the potato cakes, while the sauce could be warmed through at the last moment.

1 Place the potatoes in a pan of boiling salted water, cover and simmer for 20–25 minutes until cooked through and tender. Drain, return to the pan to dry out a little, then mash until smooth. Blanch the cabbage in a pan of boiling water for 2 minutes. Drain and quickly rinse under cold running water. Pat dry with kitchen paper.

2 Heat a tablespoon of olive oil in a frying pan and add the bacon, then sauté for a few minutes until crispy. Drain on kitchen paper and wipe out the pan. Add another tablespoon of olive oil and sauté the shallot and garlic for 3 minutes until softened but not coloured.

3 Add the cabbage to the mashed potato with the crispy bacon, shallot mixture and mixed herbs. Mix well to combine and then season to taste. Shape into four even-sized patties, toss in flour, shaking off any excess, and arrange on a flat plate or baking sheet. Cover with cling film and chill until needed.

4 Trim the monkfish and then cut into 2.5 cm/1 in medallions. Season with a little salt and press each medallion lightly into a plate of coarsely ground black pepper to coat. Arrange on a plate, cover with cling film and chill until needed.

5 To make the sauce, heat the olive oil in a pan. Add the shallot and garlic and sauté for 3 minutes until softened but not coloured. Pour in the wine and cook until evaporated. Stir in the cream and bring to the boil, then add the mustard and dill and season to taste. Reduce the heat and simmer gently until slightly reduced and thickened.

6 Meanwhile, heat two separate large frying pans. Add 1 cm/½ in of olive oil to one of the pans and then carefully lower in the potato cakes, using a fish slice. Cook for 3 minutes on each side, turning carefully with the fish slice. Add two tablespoons

salt and freshly ground black pepper

lightly dressed crisp mixed salad leaves, to serve (optional)

of olive oil to the other pan and when it is very hot, add the monkfish medallions. Cook for about 2 minutes on each side until browned and just firm when pressed.

7 Drain the potato cakes on kitchen paper and place one on each serving plate. Drain the monkfish medallions on kitchen paper and arrange on top of the potato cakes. Spoon around the mustard dill sauce and serve at once with the salad, if liked.

31 Grilled Swordfish 'Muddica'

ANTONY WORRALL
THOMPSON
FISH & SHELLFISH

Serves 4

8 tbsp fresh white breadcrumbs (very fine)

2 tbsp finely chopped fresh flat-leaf parsley

1 garlic clove, finely chopped

4 x 200 g/7 oz swordfish steaks, each about 1 cm/$\frac{1}{2}$ in thick

olive oil, for brushing

salt and freshly ground black pepper

lemon wedges, to garnish

fresh green salad, to serve

The contrast in this dish between the moist swordfish and the crispiness of the breadcrumb coating is wonderful. One of our researchers on *Saturday Kitchen* picked up the idea while on holiday in Sicily, where apparently this is the traditional way to cook swordfish. However, it would also work well with tuna or even salmon escalopes.

1 Preheat the grill. Place the breadcrumbs in a shallow dish and mix in the parsley and garlic. Season to taste. Brush the swordfish steaks with olive oil and then coat both sides in the breadcrumb mixture.

2 Arrange the coated swordfish steaks on a grill rack and cook for 3–4 minutes on each side, depending on the thickness of the fish, until cooked through, crisp and golden brown. Arrange on plates and garnish with the lemon wedges. Serve at once, with the green salad.

32 Grilled Salmon Niçoise

PAUL RANKIN
FISH & SHELLFISH

Serves 4

675 g/1½ lb salmon fillet

1 tbsp cracked black pepper-corns

2½ tbsp light olive oil

1 yellow pepper

8–12 new salad potatoes

175 g/6 oz fine green beans

2 plum tomatoes

20 pitted black olives (good quality)

2 tbsp extra virgin olive oil

2 tbsp chopped fresh flat-leaf parsley, plus extra to garnish

FOR THE DRESSING:

100 ml/3½ fl oz light olive oil

1 egg yolk

4 tsp freshly squeezed lemon juice

1½ tbsp Dijon mustard

4 canned anchovy fillets, finely chopped

1 garlic clove, crushed

5 drops Tabasco sauce

salt and freshly ground black pepper

Fresh salmon is readily available nowadays, and I've used it in a twist on the traditional salade niçoise. Here we sear the salmon as you would a steak, surround it with some chunky vegetables, and serve with an anchovy and lemon dressing: incredibly simple yet so delicious!

1 Remove the skin from the salmon fillet and discard, then cut into four equal-sized steaks. Sprinkle with the cracked black pepper and salt to taste, pressing firmly into the steaks with your hands. Coat lightly with two tablespoons of the oil, arrange on a plate and chill until ready to cook.

2 Preheat the grill. Rub the yellow pepper with the remaining half tablespoon of the oil and place on a grill rack. Cook for 20–30 minutes until the skin is well blackened and blistered, turning regularly.

3 Place the potatoes in a pan of boiling salted water, cover and simmer for 15–18 minutes just tender. Drain and leave to cool completely, then cut into slices if they seem very large. Plunge the green beans into a pan of boiling salted water and blanch for a minute or so, then drain and refresh under cold running water.

4 Remove the pepper from the grill and leave to cool, then peel off the charred skin, remove the seeds and cut into eight slices. Place in a bowl. Cut each tomato into six wedges and add to the bowl with the cooked potatoes, beans and olives. Season to taste and toss with the extra virgin olive oil and parsley. Cover with cling film and leave at room temperature.

5 To make the dressing, place the light olive oil, egg yolk, lemon juice, mustard, anchovies, garlic, Tabasco and half a teaspoon of salt in a food processor or liquidizer and pulse until smooth and emulsified.

6 To cook the salmon, heat a large heavy-based griddle pan over high heat until almost smoking. Add the salmon steaks and sear for 1–3 minutes on each side, depending on how rare you like your fish.

7 To serve, divide the vegetables among plates and arrange a salmon steak in the centre of each one. Surround with a generous drizzle of the dressing and garnish with a sprinkling of parsley.

33 Roast Sea Bream

MITCH TONKS
FISH & SHELLFISH

Serves 2–4

2 sea bream, scaled and gutted, each about 450 g/1 lb

good handful of fresh rosemary sprigs

2–3 tbsp olive oil

a little Maldon sea salt

1/2 lemon, pips removed

extra virgin olive oil, to garnish

creamed spinach with garlic and boiled new potatoes, to serve (optional)

This method of roasting with rosemary is my favourite for fish. Sea bream is easy to cook, it really needs nothing doing to it. Absolute freshness is all-important, of course. For a dinner party bream looks great presented as a whole fish dressed with a fragrant olive oil with all the rosemary branches burnt from the heat of the oven and a wonderful crisp, silver skin. Your guests can help themselves first by taking the flesh from the top of the fillet, exposing the bone, then you can remove the bone to make the bottom fillet accessible.

1 Preheat the oven to 200°C/400°F/Gas Mark 6 (fan oven 180°C from cold). Place the sea bream on a chopping board and, using a sharp knife, slash each side twice diagonally to the bone. Stick rosemary sprigs into the belly cavity and slashes – let it all hang out as this will burn, giving an extra flavour to the dish.

2 Place the sea bream in a roasting tin and drizzle with olive oil (not your best one) and then sprinkle with salt. Roast for 20 minutes until the flesh is white, the skin crisp and easily taken off the bone. Arrange on plates, add a squeeze of lemon and drizzle over a little extra virgin olive oil. Serve at once with some creamed spinach with garlic and boiled new potatoes, if liked.

34 Teriyaki Salmon

MIKE ROBINSON
FISH & SHELLFISH

Serves 2

150 g/5 oz Chinese egg noodles

1 tbsp toasted sesame oil

4 tbsp chopped fresh coriander, plus extra to garnish

grated rind and juice of 1 lime

1 tbsp vegetable oil, plus extra for brushing

1 large garlic clove, finely chopped

knob of fresh root ginger, peeled and finely chopped

1 small red chilli, seeded and finely chopped

5 tbsp dark soy sauce

2 tbsp maple syrup

2 x 100 g/4 oz salmon fillets, skinned

I first came across this dish when I was fishing on the west coast of British Columbia. A fisherman in our group cooked it for supper. Teriyaki is a Japanese dish but he sweetened it with maple syrup, which is traditional in that part of the world. The smoky sweetness really intensifies as the sauce is reduced, while the chilli gives a wonderful bite.

1 Place the noodles in a pan of boiling salted water and cook for 3 minutes until just tender. Drain and refresh quickly under cold running water. Return to the pan and stir in the sesame oil, coriander and add a teaspoon of the lime juice. Cover with a lid to keep warm.

2 Heat the vegetable oil in a heavy-based frying pan. Add the garlic, ginger and chilli and sauté for 1 minute, then add the lime rind and remaining juice, the soy sauce and maple syrup and cook for another minute until slightly reduced and sticky.

3 Meanwhile, heat a heavy-based griddle pan until smoking hot. Brush the salmon fillets with oil and add to the pan, presentation-side down. Cook for 2 minutes, then turn over and cook for another 2 minutes until just tender and lightly charred.

4 Transfer the salmon fillets to the frying pan with the teriyaki sauce, presentation-side up, with a fish slice. Spoon over and swirl around the sauce to coat the salmon completely. Arrange the noodles on plates and place a salmon fillet on each one, spooning around any remaining teriyaki sauce. Garnish with coriander and serve at once.

35 Burrida (Italian Fish Stew)

PAUL MERRETT
FISH & SHELLFISH

Serves 6–8

4 tbsp olive oil

1 onion, finely chopped

2 carrots, finely chopped

4 garlic cloves, finely chopped

3 fresh thyme sprigs, leaves stripped

1 kg/2¼ lb ripe plum tomatoes, peeled, seeded and chopped

900 ml/1½ pints fresh fish stock (from a carton is fine)

pinch of sugar

6 x 100 g/4 oz monkfish steaks (on the bone)

3 small sea bass or bream, scaled and filleted

12 squid rings, about 150 g/5oz in total

12 whole raw king prawns

12 fresh mussels, cleaned

FOR THE GARLIC CROÛTONS:

100 g/4 oz unsalted butter

6 garlic cloves, finely chopped

2 tbsp chopped fresh flat-leaf parsley

1 thin baguette

salt and freshly ground black pepper

This traditional fisherman's chowder originated in Genoa, Italy. It is a wonderfully fragrant dish with an explosion of flavours, so don't be afraid to experiment with whatever selection of fish and shellfish you can get hold of. It uses a 'cartouche', which is a paper lid that prevents too much moisture escaping and helps keep in all the flavours. Take a square of non-stick baking parchment just larger than the pan you are using. Fold it in four, then fold it over into a triangle, then over again as though you were making a cone. Measure it against the pan, from the pan's centre point to its edge, and trim it to fit. Open it out and you have a circle the size of your pan. The tomato mixture can be made a couple of days in advance and reheated before adding the fish; take care not to overcook the fish.

1 Heat the olive oil a large heavy-based frying pan. Add the onion, carrots, garlic and thyme and sauté over a low heat for about 5 minutes until the onion is softened but not coloured, stirring occasionally.

2 Stir the tomatoes into the pan and cook for another minute or so, then pour in the fish stock and bring to the boil. Season to taste and add the sugar. Reduce the heat to its lowest setting and cover with a cartouche.

3 Cook the sauce very slowly for 2 hours until well flavoured and slightly reduced. Remove from the heat and either use immediately or leave to cool and store covered with cling film in the fridge for up to 48 hours.

4 When ready to serve, preheat the grill. Bring the sauce to a simmer and add the monkfish, sea bass or bream fillets, squid, prawns and mussels. Cook gently for 5–10 minutes until all the fish is tender, the mussels have opened and the prawns are pink.

5 Meanwhile, make the garlic croûtons. Place the butter in a bowl and mix in the garlic and parsley. Season to taste. Cut the baguette on the diagonal and arrange on a grill rack. Toast on both sides and then spread with the garlic butter. Ladle the fish stew into wide-rimmed bowls and serve with the croûtons on the side.

36 Cheat's Coq Au Vin

JAMES MARTIN
POULTRY & GAME

Serves 4

1 tbsp olive oil

25 g/1 oz unsalted butter

2 red onions, thinly sliced

150 g/5 oz piece of pancetta, rind removed and chopped into lardons

4 garlic cloves, finely chopped

250 g/9 oz button mushrooms, trimmed

good pinch of dried thyme

300 ml/½ pint red wine

500 ml/18 fl oz fresh chicken stock (from a carton is fine)

8 cooked chicken pieces on the bone

150 ml/¼ pint double cream

2 tbsp chopped fresh flat-leaf parsley

salt and freshly ground black pepper

creamy mashed potato or plain boiled rice, to serve

This dish saved my life once when I was supposed to have been cooking a meal all day for that special person in my life. With half an hour to spare I rustled this up from what was in the fridge and no one was any the wiser … To make it look really authentic use a mixture of chicken breasts, thighs and legs – I promise no one will know the difference. Pancetta is an Italian cured and rolled belly pork, which to me is much tastier than British streaky bacon. Try to buy it in whole pieces from a good butcher's or Italian delicatessen, or diced in vacuum packs from a supermarket.

1 Heat a large heavy-based pan and add the oil and butter. When the butter stops foaming, add the onions, pancetta and garlic and sauté for about 5 minutes until the onions are well softened and the pancetta is sizzling. Add the mushrooms with the thyme and continue to sauté for 5 minutes until the mushrooms are tender. Pour in the wine, bring to the boil and continue to boil fast for about 5 minutes until the liquid is reduced by half.

2 Pour the stock into the pan and return to the boil. Remove the skin from the cooked chicken pieces and discard. Season the chicken pieces and add to the sauce, then reduce the heat and simmer for 5–10 minutes until the chicken is completely heated through.

3 Using a slotted spoon, transfer the chicken pieces to a warmed serving dish, cover and keep warm. Increase the heat and boil the sauce fast until reduced by half. Reduce the heat, stir in the cream and gently warm through. Pour the sauce over the chicken pieces and sprinkle over the parsley. Serve straight to the table with a separate bowl of creamy mashed potatoes or rice.

37 Chicken Bhuna with Pilau Rice

PAUL MERRETT
POULTRY & GAME

Serves 4

6 tbsp plain yoghurt

juice of 1 lemon

2 garlic cloves, finely chopped

1/2 tsp ground turmeric

1 tbsp paprika

3 cardamom pods, husks
removed and seeds crushed

1 tbsp chilli powder

1 tbsp ground cumin

1 1/2 tsp salt

4 skinless chicken breast fillets,
cut into strips

1 tbsp olive oil

1 tbsp vegetable oil

1 tsp garam masala

4 tbsp chopped fresh coriander

FOR THE PILAU RICE:

1 tbsp vegetable oil

1 onion, finely chopped

1 garlic clove, finely chopped

1/2 cinnamon stick

2 cardamom pods, lightly
crushed

1 tbsp fennel seeds

350 g/12 oz basmati rice, well
rinsed

good pinch of salt

warm naan bread, to serve

This curry recipe may have a long list of spices but don't let that put you off the preparation. The spicing is absolutely authentic and the results are well worth it. Other meats would also work well in this dish, such as strips of lean lamb, beef or even pork. The pilau rice is the perfect traditional accompaniment: fragrant and fluffy.

1 Place the yoghurt in a non-metallic bowl and add the lemon juice, garlic, turmeric, paprika, cardamom, chilli powder, cumin and salt. Mix well to combine and stir in the chicken strips. Cover with cling film and chill for at least 2 hours (or overnight is fine).

2 To make the pilau rice, heat the oil in a heavy-based pan with a lid. Add the onion and sauté for 3–4 minutes until translucent. Stir in the garlic, cinnamon, cardamom and fennel seeds, then add the rice and cook for another minute without stirring the rice.

3 Pour enough water into the pan so that it comes 2.5 cm/1 in above the level of the rice. Add the salt. Bring to the boil, cover with a lid and boil fast for 5 minutes. Remove from the heat and set aside in a warm place for 20 minutes to finish cooking – without removing the lid, or the steam will escape.

4 Meanwhile, heat a large non-stick frying pan. Add the olive and vegetable oil and fry the chicken strips for 4–5 minutes until cooked through and golden brown, turning once – you may have to do this in batches or in two pans. Sprinkle over the garam masala and coriander. Fluff the rice up with a fork and spoon on to plates with the chicken bhuna. Serve hot with the naan bread.

38 Eastern Chicken Stir-fry

MARY BERRY
POULTRY & GAME

Serves 2

1 large skinless chicken breast
fillet, cut into pencil-thin strips

1–2 tbsp olive oil

2 tsp clear honey

4 spring onions, trimmed and
thinly sliced

1 small red pepper, halved,
seeded and thinly sliced

1 small yellow pepper, halved,
seeded and thinly sliced

100 g/4 oz mangetout,
trimmed and sliced on the
diagonal

100 g/4 oz button chestnut
mushrooms, trimmed

100 g/4 oz pak choi, thickly
sliced, keeping the white and
green parts separate

1 oz/25 g salted cashew nuts

FOR THE SAUCE:

½ tsp cornflour

1 tbsp dark soy sauce

1 tbsp hoisin sauce

salt and freshly ground black
pepper

plain boiled rice, to serve
(optional)

For me, stir-fries are a wonderful way to serve fresh vegetables. The chicken and the vegetables can be prepared up to 12 hours ahead and kept in the fridge. I like to use a Caribbean honey in this recipe because it has a strong aromatic flavour that works well with the strong flavours of the soy and hoisin sauces. The high sugar content of the honey caramelizes the chicken very quickly and speeds up the cooking process, making this a speedy supper dish.

1 Heat a wok or sauté pan over a high heat until smoking hot. Season the chicken. Swirl in a tablespoon of the oil and then tip in the chicken. Drizzle over half of the honey and stir-fry for a couple of minutes until golden brown and just tender. Remove from the wok on to a plate with a slotted spoon and set aside.

2 Add the spring onions to the wok, adding a little more oil if needed – drizzle over the remaining teaspoon of honey and allow to cook for couple of minutes, tossing occasionally. Add the red and yellow peppers, mangetout, mushrooms and white part of the pak choi and toss over high heat for 2–3 minutes or until the vegetables are just tender but still crisp.

3 Meanwhile, to make the sauce, slake the cornflour with the soy sauce in a small bowl, add the hoisin sauce and mix well to combine. Return the chicken to the wok with the sauce, green parts of the pak choi and the cashew nuts. Cook for another minute or two until the sauce is thickened and bubbling. Season to taste. Spoon into Chinese-style bowls and serve immediately with separate individual bowls of rice, if liked.

39 Spicy Chicken Salad with Coriander, Mint and Noodles

PAUL RANKIN
POULTRY & GAME

Serves 4

450 g/1 lb skinless chicken breast fillets

1 garlic clove, finely chopped

1 tsp medium curry powder

1 tbsp light muscovado sugar

1 tbsp dark soy sauce

1 tbsp chilli sauce

2 tbsp shredded fresh basil

2 tbsp vegetable oil

100 g/4oz rice vermicelli

1 small red onion, very finely sliced

good handful of fresh coriander leaves

handful of fresh mint leaves

about 50 g/2 oz mixed baby salad leaves

1 red pepper, cored, seeded and cut into fine strips

FOR THE DRESSING:

1 tbsp balsamic vinegar

1 tbsp dark soy sauce

1 tsp caster sugar

1 tbsp chilli sauce

4 tbsp vegetable oil

Don't let the list of ingredients put you off. Essentially this is a simple salad that can be whipped up in very little time. Coriander and mint complement each other, and the spicy chicken, beautifully. This dish would work equally well with prawns or fresh white crab meat.

1 Cut the chicken into 2.5 cm/1 in strips and place in a shallow non-metallic dish. Blend the garlic in a bowl with the curry powder, muscovado sugar, soy, chilli sauce, basil and vegetable oil. Pour over the chicken, mixing to combine, then cover with cling film and chill for at least 15 minutes (or overnight is fine).

2 When you are ready to serve, preheat the grill to high. Arrange the marinated chicken strips on a foil-lined grill rack and cook for 4–5 minutes without turning. Remove from the grill and cover with foil to finish cooking and keep warm.

3 Meanwhile, place the rice vermicelli in a large bowl, and cover with boiling water. Leave until soft, about 10 minutes. Place the sliced onion in iced water for 2–3 minutes – this will make it crisp and mellow the flavour a little. Drain both the vermicelli and onion well and place in a large bowl. Add the coriander, mint, salad leaves and the red pepper.

4 To make the dressing, place the balsamic vinegar in a small bowl with the soy, sugar, chilli sauce and vegetable oil. Whisk to combine. To serve, add the chicken strips with any juices and the dressing to the salad. Toss gently with your hands to combine and arrange on plates to serve.

40 Chicken Forestière

MIKE ROBINSON
POULTRY & GAME

Serves 2

40 g/1½ oz dried morel mushrooms

350 g/12 oz floury potatoes, chopped

about 50 g/2 oz unsalted butter

300 ml/½ pint double cream

2 tbsp chopped fresh sage

2 skinless chicken breast fillets

50 g/2 oz seasoned flour

2 shallots, finely chopped

1 garlic clove, crushed

150 ml/¼ pint dry white wine

about 50 ml/2 fl oz Cognac

salt and freshly ground black pepper

This classic French dish from the Burgundy region with its rich, creamy sauce is not for the faint-hearted. Morels have the most fantastic intense 'mushroomy' flavour and grow wild in both field and woodland. They look very different to normal mushrooms because instead of a cap they have an upright body that is hollow inside, as is the stem. This recipe uses dried morels.

1 Place the morels in a small bowl and pour over enough hot water to cover. Set aside to soak for 30 minutes, then drain, reserving the soaking liquid.

2 Place the potatoes in a pan of boiling salted water for 20–25 minutes or until completely tender. Drain and then mash until smooth. Beat in a knob of the butter, a good splash of cream and the sage. Season to taste and cover with a lid to keep warm until ready to serve.

3 Heat two heavy-based frying pans. Cut the chicken fillets into strips. Place the flour on a flat plate and lightly dust the chicken strips, shaking off any excess. Add a knob of the butter to one of the pans and once it has stopped foaming add the chicken strips. Sauté for 1–2 minutes until sealed and lightly browned.

4 Add a knob of butter to the other frying pan and then tip in the sautéed chicken strips. Continue to cook for another 3–4 minutes until completely tender and cooked through, tossing occasionally.

5 Meanwhile, add another knob of butter to the first frying pan and tip in the shallots, garlic and drained morels. Sauté for 30 seconds and then add a good splash of wine and the Cognac to deglaze, scraping the bottom of the pan with a wooden spoon to remove any sediment. Ignite with a match to flambé.

6 Stir the remaining cream into the morel mixture in the pan. Simmer for a couple of minutes until well reduced and thickened. Season to taste. If you find that you have reduced the sauce too much simply loosen it with a little of the reserved soaking liquid from the morels.

7 Place a good dollop of the sage mash in the centre of each plate and arrange the chicken strips around it. Drizzle around the morel sauce and serve at once.

41 Preserved-lemon Roast Chicken with Sweet Potato and Rosemary Mash

SILVANA FRANCO
POULTRY & GAME

Serves 4

1.5 kg/3 lb oven-ready free-range chicken

6 garlic cloves, not peeled

4 fresh thyme sprigs

4 small preserved or pickled lemons, in quarters

knob of unsalted butter

FOR THE MASH:

2 kg/4½ lb sweet potatoes, peeled and thickly sliced (orange-fleshed, if possible)

1 tbsp olive oil

1 tbsp chopped fresh rosemary

5–6 tbsp crème fraîche

salt and freshly ground black pepper

To preserve your own lemons, cut them into quarters and layer in a sterilized Kilner jar with coarse sea salt, a couple of red chillies and a few bay leaves – you can be relaxed about quantities. The salt draws the moisture out of the lemons and makes the skin and pith edible. Leave for a month, by which time the lemons will have lost all their bitterness and have an intriguing mellowness. I think of them as a pickle and love eating them with cheese and crackers.

1 Preheat the oven to 200°C/400°F/Gas Mark 6 (fan oven 180°C from cold). To joint the chicken, place on a chopping board and, holding the breast firmly, cut off the end joint of the drumsticks and the parson's nose. Cut along one side of the breastbone from the body cavity to the neck cavity. Spread open and cut along both sides of the backbone to remove it. Lay the chicken halves, skin-side up, on the board and cut diagonally between the breast and leg joints. Cut in half again to make eight portions, discarding the carcass or using it for stock.

2 Arrange the chicken pieces snugly in a roasting tin and tuck in the garlic cloves, thyme sprigs and lemon quarters. Season generously and dot with the butter. Roast for 40 minutes or until the chicken pieces are cooked through and golden brown.

3 Meanwhile, place the sweet potatoes in a separate roasting tin and drizzle over the olive oil. Add the rosemary and season to taste, then toss until everything is well coated. Roast for about 30 minutes or until the sweet potatoes are tender and golden. Roughly mash the sweet potatoes in the tin and then beat in enough of the crème fraîche with a wooden spoon to make a mash.

4 Divide the chicken pieces between 4 plates, making sure that everyone gets some garlic and preserved lemon. Arrange the sweet potato and rosemary mash on the side and serve at once.

42 Baby Chicken in a Cider Sauce

GENNARO CONTALDO
POULTRY & GAME

Serves 2–4

4 garlic cloves, peeled

2 tbsp rinsed capers

2 tsp extra virgin olive oil

2 baby chickens (poussins)

6 tbsp olive oil

2 fresh rosemary branches, leaves stripped

120 ml/4 fl oz white wine

120 ml/4 fl oz cider vinegar

salt and freshly ground black pepper

lightly dressed fresh green salad, to serve (optional)

Baby chickens (poussins) are much more tender than fully matured ones. They also look more attractive when served. You can choose whether to serve a whole one to each person, or one between two, depending on appetites. I find that if you are serving a starter and accompaniments, then one poussin between two people is enough.

1 Place two of the garlic cloves in a pestle and mortar with the capers, one teaspoon of salt and the extra virgin olive oil. Add a good grinding of pepper and pound to a pulp. Set aside until ready to use.

2 Using poultry shears or sharp kitchen scissors, cut each poussin along the back, down each side of the backbone, then remove and discard the backbone to open them up like a butterfly. Snip the wishbone in half and open out the poussin, then snip out the ribs. Turn over, so it is skin-side up, and press down firmly on the breastbone with the heel of your hand to flatten it out. Trim off any excess skin, wash under cold running water and pat dry with kitchen paper.

3 Spread the garlic paste evenly over the flesh side of each poussin, then fold each one back over and secure the opening with cocktail sticks, weaving them in and out. Season generously. Heat the ordinary olive oil in a large frying pan with a lid, add the poussins, then reduce the heat slightly and cook until golden brown on all sides. Then cover and cook gently for 20 minutes or until the poussins are completely tender.

4 Meanwhile, place the remaining garlic in the pestle and mortar with the rosemary and pound to a paste. Gradually add the wine and cider vinegar, mixing to combine.

5 When the poussins are tender, increase the heat and stir in the garlic mixture. Simmer until reduced by half, stirring continuously. Arrange the poussins on plates and spoon over the sauce. Serve hot with salad, if liked.

43 Pot-roasted Guinea Fowl with Onion Confit

PAUL MERRETT
POULTRY & GAME

Serves 2

1 whole oven-ready guinea fowl

40 g/1½ oz unsalted butter

1 onion, halved

300 ml/½ pint fresh chicken stock (from a carton is fine)

olive oil, for frying

1 small leek, chopped

1 carrot, chopped

2 celery sticks, chopped

1 fresh thyme sprig, leaves stripped

1 small garlic clove, finely chopped

4 tbsp white wine

200 g/7 oz peas (fresh or frozen)

1 tbsp chopped fresh chervil

1 tbsp chopped fresh tarragon

salt and freshly ground black pepper

For a rich, tasty and memorable meal, look no further – the depth of flavour achieved by pot-roasting the guinea fowl is fantastic, especially when you consider that it only takes 15 minutes in the oven. Guinea fowl has a richer and more gamey flavour than chicken, but take care not to overcook it as it is a very lean bird and can dry out.

1 Preheat the oven to 160°C/325°F/Gas Mark 3 (fan oven 140°C from cold). To cut the guinea fowl into portions, place on a chopping board and, holding the breast firmly, cut off the end joint of the drumsticks and the parson's nose. Cut along one side of the breastbone from the body cavity to the neck cavity. Spread open and cut along both sides of the backbone to remove it. Lay the guinea fowl halves, skin-side up, on the board and cut diagonally between the breast and leg joints. Cut the legs in half again between the drumsticks and thighs, discarding the carcass or using it for stock.

2 To make the onion confit, heat a small ovenproof pan and add 25 g/1 oz of the butter. Once it is foaming, add the onion halves, cut-side down. Cook for a minute or two until really golden brown. Add four tablespoons of the stock and cover tightly with foil. Transfer to the top shelf of the oven and roast for 25–30 minutes or until completely tender but still holding their shape.

3 Heat a large heavy-based casserole dish with a lid. Add a little oil and then add half of the guinea fowl portions, skin-side down. Cook for a few minutes on each side until golden brown. Transfer to a plate and repeat with the remaining portions, adding a little more oil if necessary.

4 Add a little more oil to the pan and tip in the leek, carrot, celery, thyme and garlic. Sauté for 4–5 minutes until softened but not coloured. Remove from the heat and arrange the guinea fowl portions on top, then pour around the wine. Cover with a lid and cook on the second shelf of the oven for about 15 minutes or until the guinea fowl is completely tender. The breasts may be ready a few minutes before the leg meat, in which case remove and keep warm.

5 Meanwhile, make the pea purée. Place the remaining stock in a small pan and bring it to the boil. Add the peas, the remaining knob of butter and the herbs and simmer for 2–3 minutes until tender. Blend to a coarse purée with a hand-held blender. Season to taste. When the onion confit is cooked, carefully remove the centre of each onion to leave a shell. (Eating the centre of the onion is the chef's kitchen privilege.) Fill the onion shells with the pea purée and arrange on plates with the guinea fowl. Serve at once with some of the cooking juices from the guinea fowl.

44 Honeyed Duck Confit with Creamy Mash and Crispy Seaweed

JAMES MARTIN
POULTRY & GAME

Serves 2

2 confit duck legs (home-made or from a tin or jar is fine)

4 tbsp clear honey

3 tbsp olive oil

2–3 fresh thyme sprigs, leaves stripped

300 g/11 oz potatoes, cut into small chunks

250 ml/9 fl oz fresh chicken stock (from a carton is fine)

100 ml/3½ fl oz red wine

3 tbsp milk

small knob of unsalted butter

50 g/2 oz crispy seaweed

salt and freshly ground black pepper

This is about as fussy as I get with food, but what a superb dish. Crispy seaweed is now readily available in supermarkets in cook-chill packets, often in the Chinese section. It is normally made from spring cabbage or spring greens, not seaweed at all. Make sure you keep all the duck fat as it is fantastic for making roast potatoes or frying an egg and will keep indefinitely, covered, in the fridge.

1 Preheat the oven to 180°C/350°F/Gas Mark 4 (fan oven 160°C from cold). Scrape the fat from the duck legs and place them in a small roasting tin; reserve the fat. Whisk together the honey and oil in a small bowl and smear all over the duck legs. Sprinkle over the thyme leaves and roast for 20 minutes until the duck is completely heated through, basting every 5 minutes or so.

2 Meanwhile, place the potatoes in a pan of boiling salted water and cook for 15–20 minutes until tender. Place the stock in a pan with the wine and bring to the boil, then boil fast until reduced by two-thirds. Season to taste.

3 Drain the potatoes and return to the pan to dry out a little. Meanwhile, heat the milk in a small pan or in the microwave. Mash the potatoes with a fork, gradually beating in the hot milk and the butter. Season to taste.

4 Spoon the mash on to the centre of plates, sprinkle over the seaweed and sit the duck legs on top. Scrape any meaty bits from the bottom of the roasting tin and sprinkle on top. Pour over the reduced wine sauce and serve immediately.

45 Duck with Redcurrant and Red Wine Sauce

MIKE ROBINSON
POULTRY & GAME

Serves 2

2 duck breasts, well trimmed (skin on)

2 shallots, finely chopped

1 garlic clove, finely chopped

pinch of chopped fresh thyme

5 cherry tomatoes, halved

2 tbsp balsamic vinegar

about 75 ml/3 fl oz red wine

25 g/1 oz unsalted butter, diced and chilled

3 tbsp redcurrant jelly

salt and freshly ground black pepper

crusty French bread and lightly dressed green salad, to serve (optional)

The contrast in this dish between the succulent duck and the sweet redcurrant sauce is wonderful – the acidity in the fruit cuts through the richness of the meat. Obviously, fresh redcurrants would work extremely well instead of the jelly – you'll need about 50 g/2 oz in total. For a dinner party, try serving it with gratin dauphinois and some steamed purple-stemmed broccoli tossed in a knob of butter.

1 Preheat the oven to 180°C/350°F/Gas Mark 4 (fan oven 160°C from cold). Heat an ovenproof frying pan over a moderate heat. Using a sharp knife, lightly score the skin of each duck breast in a criss-cross pattern. When the pan is hot, add the duck breasts, skin-side down, and cook for 2 minutes until the skin is golden. Turn over and cook for another minute or so to seal, then transfer to the oven and cook for 10 minutes for medium-rare, or give them a few minutes longer if you prefer your duck better done.

2 Remove the duck breasts from the oven and transfer them to a warm plate, then allow to rest in a warm place while you prepare the sauce. Carefully drain the excess fat from the frying pan. Add the shallots, garlic, thyme and tomatoes and sauté for a couple of minutes until the shallots are beginning to soften.

3 Deglaze the pan with the balsamic vinegar and red wine, scraping the bottom with a wooden spoon to remove any sediment and allowing the mixture to reduce down a little. Whisk in the butter and redcurrant jelly until well combined, and season to taste. Carve the duck breasts on the diagonal and arrange on plates. Drizzle around the sauce and serve at once with some crusty French bread and salad, if liked.

46 Fillet of Beef en Croûte with Creamed Spinach

PAUL MERRETT
MEAT

Serves 4

50 g/2 oz plain flour, plus extra for dusting

2 eggs, plus 1 egg white

150 ml/¼ pint milk

2 tbsp mixed fresh herbs, such as chervil, tarragon and chives

olive oil, for frying

350 g/12 oz beef fillet (in one piece)

1 tbsp prepared English mustard

225 g/8 oz ready-made puff pastry, thawed if frozen

50 g/2 oz spinach, tough stalks removed

8 tbsp double cream

salt and freshly ground black pepper

Food trends come and go but this is one recipe that has stood the test of time and once you've taken your first bite you'll understand why. This dish is perfect for a dinner party as it can be prepared several hours in advance, ready to be popped into the oven as the first course is being served. The quality of the beef is essential to the success of this dish. It is well worth visiting your butcher and asking his advice.

1 To make the pancakes, sift the flour and a pinch of salt into a bowl, and make a well in the centre. Break in one of the eggs and add a little of the milk. Mix the liquid ingredients together, then gradually beat in the flour until smooth. Beat in the remaining milk to obtain the consistency of single cream. Add the herbs. Cover with cling film and leave for 20 minutes to allow the batter to rest.

2 To cook the pancakes, heat a large heavy-based frying pan. When the pan is hot, smear with the minimum of oil. Pour in a small amount of the batter and swirl it around until it is evenly and thinly spread over the bottom of the pan. Cook for 1 minute until the edges start to curl away from the sides of the pan. Flip over and cook for another 30 seconds or so until lightly golden. Transfer to a plate and cover with a square of non-stick parchment paper. Repeat until you have four pancakes in total.

3 Preheat the oven to 180°C/350°F/Gas Mark 4 (fan oven 160°C from cold). Heat a little oil in a non-stick frying pan. Season the beef. When the pan is hot, add the beef and quickly seal all over. Remove from the pan, place on a plate and allow to cool completely. Place the egg white in a bowl and beat in the mustard until well combined. Brush all over the cooled beef fillet and wrap in a single layer of the pancakes, cutting them to fit as necessary.

4 On a lightly floured work surface roll out the pastry to at least six times the surface area of the beef. Cover the beef lengthways with a 1 cm/½ in overlap. Trim the ends of the pastry to 5 cm/2 in longer than the beef fillet, then neatly fold in the ends, dampening the edges to seal. Place the pastry-wrapped beef fillet seam-side down on a large, non-stick baking sheet. Break the remaining egg into a small bowl and season. Beat with a fork and then use to brush all over the pastry. Bake for about 12 minutes or until the pastry is puffed up and golden brown. Remove from the oven to a carving board and allow to rest for 5 minutes.

5 Meanwhile, prepare the creamed spinach. Blanch the spinach in a large pan of boiling salted water until wilted, then drain and quickly refresh in cold water. Drain well, pat dry with kitchen paper and finely chop. Place the cream in a pan and simmer gently until reduced by half, stirring occasionally. Stir in the spinach and allow to just warm through. Season to taste. Carve the beef en croûte into slices and arrange on plates with the creamed spinach to serve.

47 Beef Rolls in Tomato Ragù

GENNARO CONTALDO
MEAT

Serves 6

12 small thin sirloin steaks

25 g/1 oz freshly grated Parmesan

4 garlic cloves, finely chopped

handful of fresh flat-leaf parsley, torn

6 tbsp olive oil

150 ml/¼ pint red wine

1 onion, very finely chopped

1 celery stick, very finely chopped

2 tbsp tomato purée

400 ml/14 fl oz lukewarm water

2 x 400 g/14 oz cans chopped tomatoes

handful of fresh basil leaves, torn

salt and freshly ground black pepper

tagliatelle or large rigatoni and lightly dressed fresh green salad, to serve

This recipe takes me back to childhood Sunday lunches. My aunt Maria was the 'queen' of this dish and would spend the entire morning checking, stirring and making sure it was just right. It is traditionally made every Sunday in all regions of southern Italy: the tomato sauce is used to flavour pasta for the *primo* (pasta course) and the meat is eaten as a *secondo* (main course).

1 Arrange the steaks on a chopping board and flatten them with a meat tenderizer (if you don't have one, place a flat wooden spatula over the meat and bash with the palm of your hand). Season and then sprinkle over the Parmesan, garlic and parsley. Roll each slice up tightly and secure well with cocktail sticks.

2 To make the sauce, heat the olive oil in a large pan. When it is hot, reduce the heat and add the beef rolls and seal well on all sides. Increase the heat again, pour in the wine and allow to simmer until reduced by half. Transfer the beef rolls to a plate and set aside.

3 Add the onion to the pan with the celery, stirring to combine, then continue to cook until all the wine has nearly evaporated. Stir the tomato purée in a jug with the lukewarm water to combine. Return the beef rolls to the pan and pour in the tomato purée mixture and chopped tomatoes. Season to taste and stir in the basil.

4 Reduce the heat, cover partially with a lid so that some of the steam can escape and cook gently for 2 hours until the sauce has thickened and reduced and the beef rolls are completely tender, stirring occasionally. Season to taste. Serve the tomato sauce with some tagliatelle or large rigatoni, then serve the beef rolls as a main course with some salad.

48 Baked Lamb with Herbs and Peppers

MIKE ROBINSON
MEAT

Serves 4–6

50 g/2 oz bunch of fresh mixed herbs, such as rosemary, oregano, thyme and marjoram

4 large garlic cloves, finely chopped

about 3 tbsp olive oil, plus extra for drizzling

1 tsp Maldon sea salt

2 tsp whole black peppercorns

1 lamb shoulder, boned but with knuckle left in

2 red peppers, halved, seeded and sliced

450 g/1 lb baby new potatoes

350 g/12 oz parsnips, cut into chunks

350 g/12 oz carrots, cut into chunks

1 lemon, sliced

1 tsp softened unsalted butter

1 tsp plain flour

about 50 ml/2 fl oz red wine

salt and freshly ground black pepper

I first came up with this way of cooking lamb when I had to cater for a large number at an outdoor party. The lamb foil parcels were baked in coals in a deep pit in the garden for several hours, filling the air with the irresistible smell of roasting meat and herbs. I like to use a shoulder of lamb with the knuckle left in so that you have something to hold on to when you come to carve – most good butchers should be happy to do this for you.

1 Preheat the oven to 220°C/425°F/Gas Mark 7 (fan oven 200°C from cold). Strip the leaves from the herbs and place in a pestle and mortar. Add half the garlic and a few drops of oil and pound into a coarse paste. Add the sea salt and peppercorns and continue to pound until well combined.

2 Lay the lamb on a clean work surface skin-side down. Using a sharp knife, slash the meat deeply at 0.5 cm/¼ in intervals. Rub two-thirds of the herb paste into the cuts and arrange an even layer of the red peppers on top. Roll up and secure with string at 2.5 cm/1 in intervals: this helps to keep the joint together while it's cooking. Rub some of the remaining herb paste all over the skin of the joint.

3 Layer up four sheets of foil and use to wrap the lamb joint into a secure parcel. Place in a large roasting tin and cook for 30 minutes. Meanwhile, lay another large sheet of foil on the work surface and pile up the new potatoes, parsnips, carrots, remaining garlic, the lemon slices and any of the remaining herb paste on one side. Drizzle over enough oil to barely coat everything and season to taste, then fold over to enclose. Secure into a large envelope shape. Remove the lamb parcel from the oven and place the vegetable parcel alongside it in the roasting tin. Roast for another hour or until the lamb is completely tender and the vegetables are all cooked through and slightly caramelized.

4 Remove the foil parcels from the oven and carefully open the lamb parcel. Strain all the cooking juices into a small pan and bring to a simmer. Meanwhile, mix the butter and flour into a paste and whisk bit by bit into the sauce. Add the red wine and simmer until reduced to a sauce-like consistency, stirring constantly. Season to taste. Carve the lamb into slices and arrange on serving plates. Open the foil parcel of vegetables and divide among the plates. Finally drizzle around some of the lamb gravy to serve.

49 Noisettes of Lamb with Puff Pizza and Roast Garlic and Basil Cream

PAUL RANKIN
MEAT

Serves 4

2 tbsp vegetable oil

10 garlic cloves, not peeled

about 450 ml/³/₄ pint boiling water

550 g/1¹/₄ lb lamb loin (full length – all in one piece)

4 tbsp white wine, lamb stock or water

200 ml/7 fl oz double cream

2 tbsp finely shredded basil, plus extra leaves to garnish

1–2 tsp Dijon mustard

50 g/2 oz unsalted butter

200 g/7 oz fresh spinach, picked over and cleaned

FOR THE PUFF PIZZA:

150–175 g/5–6 oz ready-made puff pastry, thawed if frozen

a little plain flour, for dusting

15 g/¹/₂ oz unsalted butter, plus extra for greasing

¹/₂ courgette, thinly sliced

¹/₂ red pepper, seeded and thinly sliced

¹/₂ red onion, thinly sliced

4 button mushrooms, sliced

1 egg yolk, lightly beaten

1 heaped tbsp freshly grated Parmesan

salt and freshly ground black pepper

Stunning and simple – need I say more? Oh, and it tastes great too!

1 To make the pizza, roll out the pastry on a lightly floured board so it is 0.5 cm/¹/₄ in thick and then chill in the fridge for at least 30 minutes. Meanwhile, preheat the oven to 190°C/375°F/Gas Mark 5 (fan oven 170°C from cold). Cut a 20 cm/8 in circle from the pastry and prick the whole surface evenly with a fork. Place on a greased baking sheet and cook for 10–15 minutes until puffed up and lightly golden. Remove from the oven and leave to cool a little.

2 While the pastry is baking, make the pizza topping. Heat the butter in a frying pan and sauté the courgette, red pepper, onion and mushrooms for a few minutes until just wilted but not fully cooked. Season to taste and leave to cool a little.

3 Meanwhile, prepare the lamb. Heat half the oil in a heavy-based frying pan. Add the garlic cloves and cook for a minute or two until heated through, tossing regularly. Tip into a bowl and pour over enough boiling water to cover completely, cover with cling film and set aside to soften, about 20 minutes. Season the lamb loin generously, pressing the seasoning on to the surface. Heat the remaining oil in the pan until it is nearly smoking. Add the lamb and cook over high heat until well browned all over – this should take about 10 minutes, by which time the lamb will be cooked medium-rare.

4 To finish the pizza, reduce the oven temperature to 180°C/350°F/Gas Mark 4 (fan oven 160°C). Brush the pastry with a little of the egg yolk to stop it absorbing excess liquid from the vegetables, then toss the rest of the egg yolk with the vegetables and Parmesan. Spread the tossed vegetables evenly over the pastry and return to the oven for about 10 minutes until the pastry is puffed and golden brown and the vegetables are cooked. Cut into wedges and keep warm.

5 Transfer the lamb to a warm plate and cover with foil. Pour off the fat from the pan and add the wine, stock or water. Scrape in the caramelized meat juices from the bottom of the pan as the liquid comes to the boil.

6 Squeeze the garlic from their skins – they should pop out easily – and mash lightly with a fork. Stir into the pan with the cream and bring to a fast boil, then remove from the heat and stir in the basil and mustard.

7 Heat a large heavy-based frying pan over a medium heat. Add half of the butter, and when it has foamed and then subsided, toss in the spinach. Cook for 1–2 minutes, keeping the spinach leaves moving around with a spatula, and season with a little salt. Add the remaining butter, tossing to combine, and season to taste.

8 Carve the rested lamb into slices, mixing any juices into the sauce. Arrange the slices on plates with a little sautéed spinach and spoon the sauce around it. Add slices of the vegetable puff pizza, garnished with the basil leaves, to serve.

50 Lamb Cutlets with Thyme and Sage Crust

CURTIS STONE
MEAT

Serves 2

75 g/3 oz unsalted butter

8 slices white bread, crusts removed

4 tbsp chopped fresh mixed herbs (such as thyme, sage, flat-leaf parsley and rosemary)

6-bone best end of lamb or 6 lamb cutlets

olive oil, for frying

2–3 tbsp Dijon mustard

salt and freshly ground black pepper

round of sweet potato gratin (see recipe p. 104) and thin lamb gravy, to serve

British lamb is wonderful, especially if you can track down some of the native breeds that the better supermarkets are now stocking. It's at its best from the end of May until mid-September, after which it develops a more pronounced mutton-like flavour. Don't be tempted to pat down the breadcrumbs on the cutlets – just leave them in a loose pile.

1 Preheat the oven to 200°C/400°F/Gas Mark 6 (fan oven 180°C from cold). Melt the butter in a small pan or in the microwave. Place the bread in a food processor or liquidizer and whiz into breadcrumbs, then tip into a bowl and stir in the herbs. Season to taste and slowly add the melted butter until just combined. Set aside.

2 If using a rack of lamb, cut into six individual cutlets. Heat a frying pan until searing hot. Add a thin layer of olive oil and quickly seal the cutlets on both sides – you may have to do this in batches depending on the size of your pan. Transfer to a roasting tin.

3 Brush each cutlet with a little of the mustard and sprinkle about a tablespoon of the breadcrumb mixture on top of each one. Roast for 3–5 minutes, depending on the size of your chops, or until the lamb is tender and the breadcrumbs are golden brown.

4 Place a round of the sweet potato gratin off centre on each plate. Arrange three of the cutlets alongside each one. Drizzle with a little of the lamb gravy and serve at once.

51 Lamb Koftas with Cucumber and Mint Yoghurt

MIKE ROBINSON
MEAT

Serves 2

2 tsp cumin seeds

1 tsp coriander seeds

2 tbsp pine nuts

small bunch of fresh coriander, chopped (stalks and leaves)

1 red chilli, seeded and chopped

2 tsp ground turmeric

good pinch of ground cinnamon

300 g/11 oz lean minced lamb

grated rind and juice of 2 limes

FOR THE MINT YOGHURT:

1 mini cucumber, halved and seeds removed

100 g/4 oz Greek strained yoghurt

2 tbsp chopped fresh mint

rind and juice of 1 lemon

salt and freshly ground black pepper

chopped fresh coriander, to garnish

There are variations of these kebabs across the whole of the eastern Mediterranean and right up to northern India. The succulently seasoned mixture of finely minced lamb is a winning combination with the cooling mint yoghurt. I also like to eat them with warmed pitta bread and a tomato, onion and feta cheese salad. If you want to use bamboo skewers, soak them in water for 30 minutes first or they will scorch in the oven.

1 Heat a small heavy-based frying pan. Add the cumin, coriander seeds and pine nuts and cook until lightly toasted, tossing occasionally. Tip into a pestle and mortar or mini blender and add the coriander, chilli, turmeric and cinnamon. Pound or blend to a fine paste. Tip into a bowl and add the minced lamb, lime rind and juice. Season to taste and mix well to combine.

2 Divide the lamb mixture into four equal portions and roll these into narrow cylinders about 20 cm/8 in long. Thread a long, flat, metal skewer gently through the middle of each one and gently squeeze the meat around the skewer. Arrange on a plate, cover loosely with cling film and leave to rest for at least 10 minutes to firm up – they will be fine for up to 12 hours.

3 Preheat the oven to 200°C/400°F/Gas Mark 6 (fan oven 180°C from cold). Heat a large ovenproof griddle pan until smoking hot. Cook the lamb koftas for a minute or two on each side until sealed and lightly charred. Transfer to the oven and cook for another 8–10 minutes or until cooked through and completely tender.

4 Meanwhile, make the mint yoghurt. Grate the cucumber and place in a clean tea towel, then squeeze out all the excess water. Place in a bowl and beat in the yoghurt, mint, lemon rind and juice and season to taste. Arrange the lamb koftas on plates with a good dollop of the mint yoghurt. Scatter over the coriander to garnish and serve at once.

52 Irish Stew

RICHARD CORRIGAN
MEAT

Serves 4

1 kg/2¼ lb scrag end or neck of lamb

2 carrots, roughly chopped

1 large onion, roughly chopped

2 celery sticks, roughly chopped

1 leek, trimmed and roughly chopped

2–3 garlic cloves, peeled

1 large bay leaf

1 large fresh thyme sprig

150 g/5 oz small carrots

150 g/5 oz baby or pickling onions

1 large floury potato, finely diced, about 275 g/10 oz in total

2 spring onions, thinly sliced, to garnish

a little chopped fresh flat-leaf parsley, to garnish

salt and freshly ground black pepper

I could never tire of a bowl of steaming hot stew. To make sure it's light and not greasy I always first blanch the meat in boiling water. It's the attention to detail that makes this dish one of the world's great classics – well, to my mind at any rate. This is the version I have developed over the years and the main ingredients are still the same as my mum uses, and her mother used before her. Irish stew was traditionally made when people had lots of potatoes and wanted to cook their supper all in one pot over the open peat fire.

1 Using a sharp, thin boning knife, remove as much meat from the lamb bones as possible. Chop into small pieces and place in a bowl. Cover with cling film and chill until needed.

2 Place the lamb bones in a large stockpot. Add the roughly chopped carrots, onion, celery, leek, garlic and herbs. Cover with at least 4 litres/7 pints of cold water. Bring to the boil, season lightly and then simmer gently, uncovered, for about 2 hours until reduced by nearly two-thirds – you'll need 1.2 litres/2 pints of lovely, sweet stock in total. Skim off any scum or grease that rises to the surface with a large tablespoon. Strain the stock through a fine sieve into a large jug and ideally leave to cool and chill overnight so that you can scrape off any fat that has settled on the top.

3 To make the stew, place the lamb pieces in a large pan with a lid and cover with cold water. Bring slowly to the boil, skimming off any scum, then quickly drain into a colander in the sink and rinse under cold running water. This scalding removes fat. Return the meat to the pan and cover with the stock. Bring to the boil, then reduce the heat and simmer for about 30 minutes, partially covered with a lid.

4 Meanwhile, cut the baby carrots into small chunks or shape into neat 'barrels'. Peel the baby onions – it helps to blanch them in boiling water for a minute first. Add the baby carrots and onions to the simmering lamb and cook for 5 minutes; then add the potato and simmer for another 10–15 minutes until the potato starts to dissolve into the stew and thicken it. Season to taste and ladle into wide-rimmed bowls. Garnish with the spring onions and parsley and serve at once.

53 Pork with Pesto and Parma Ham

Meat

MIKE ROBINSON
MEAT

Serves 2

50 g/2 oz pine nuts

large bunch of fresh basil, leaves stripped

2 fresh sage leaves

1 garlic clove, peeled

100 g/4 oz pecorino cheese, finely grated

about 75 ml/3 fl oz olive oil

400 g/14 oz piece of pork fillet, trimmed

6 thin slices Parma ham, about 100 g/4 oz in total

FOR THE RÖSTI:

25 g/1 oz unsalted butter

2 large potatoes, preferably Maris Piper

1 egg, beaten

olive oil, for frying

salt and freshly ground black pepper

I picked up this idea while working in a hotel in Tasmania and just love the robust combination of the salty Parma ham, pungent pesto and tender pork. Using the handle of a wooden spoon to make a hole in the pork fillet may seem a bit extreme but it works brilliantly – you just need to use a bit of force to push the handle through.

1 Preheat the oven to 200°C/400°F/Gas Mark 6 (fan oven 180°C from cold). To make the pesto, heat a small heavy-based frying pan. Add the pine nuts and cook until golden brown, tossing occasionally. Tip out on to a plate and leave to cool completely. Place in a food processor or liquidizer with the basil, sage, garlic and pecorino. Blend briefly and then pour in enough of the olive oil through the feeder tube to make a thick purée. Season to taste.

2 Place the pork fillet on a chopping board with the thickest part facing you and ram the handle of a large wooden spoon down the length of it. Fill a piping bag fitted with a 2 cm/³⁄₄ in plain nozzle with the pesto and pipe it into the hole made in the fillet. Smear the remaining pesto all over the fillet, then wrap it up in the Parma ham. If it's not keeping together properly, tie it with butcher's string at 2.5 cm/1 in intervals. Place in a roasting tin and cover with foil. Bake for 15 minutes, then remove the foil and cook for another 5 minutes until cooked through and the Parma ham is crispy. Remove from the oven and leave to rest for 5 minutes in a warm place.

3 Meanwhile, make the rösti. Heat a large heavy-based frying pan. Melt the butter in a small pan or in the microwave. Leave to cool. Peel the potatoes and coarsely grate. Squeeze out the excess moisture with a clean tea towel and place in a bowl. Season generously and add the melted butter and enough beaten egg to bind, stirring to combine. Add a thin film of oil to the pan and then spoon in six small mounds of the potato mixture. Cook over a low heat for about 20 minutes, turning once until crisp and golden brown. Drain on kitchen paper. Carve the rested pork into slices and arrange on plates with the rösti to serve.

54 Char Sui Roasted Pork with Asian Wok-tossed Vegetables

CURTIS STONE
MEAT

Serves 2

1 pork fillet, well trimmed

vegetable oil, for frying

1 large shallot, finely chopped

1 small garlic clove, finely chopped

knob of root ginger, peeled and finely chopped

150 g/5 oz broccoli florets

1 courgette, sliced

1 carrot, sliced

$\frac{1}{4}$ red, yellow and green pepper, seeded and sliced

400 g/14 oz pak choi, cut across into 2.5 cm/1 in wide strips

3 tbsp dark soy sauce

1 tbsp oyster sauce

1 tsp toasted sesame oil

FOR THE MARINADE:

200 ml/7 fl oz char sui marinade

3 tbsp clear honey

1 garlic clove, crushed

2 cm/$\frac{3}{4}$ in piece of fresh root ginger, peeled and finely chopped

1 tbsp dark soy sauce

Char sui is a traditional Chinese marinade that is available in jars from good delicatessens and Chinese supermarkets. If you want to make your own, combine 50 g/2 oz of caster sugar with three table-spoons of sweet sherry, two tablespoons of dark soy sauce, 120 ml/4 fl oz of hoisin sauce, two teaspoons of finely chopped fresh root ginger, half a teaspoon each of Chinese five-spice powder and red food colouring and a teaspoon of salt. Use as described below.

1 Place the char sui marinade in a shallow non-metallic dish and stir in the honey, garlic, ginger and soy sauce until well combined. Add the pork fillet, turning to coat, then cover the dish with cling film. Set aside to marinate in the fridge for at least 12 hours – up to 24 hours is best.

2 Preheat the oven to 180°C/350°F/Gas Mark 4 (fan oven 160°C from cold). Heat a large ovenproof frying pan. Add a thin film of oil and then quickly seal the pork on all sides. Roast for 5–10 minutes, depending on the thickness of your fillet, until tender and caramelized to a golden brown. Remove from the oven to a carving board and leave to rest for 2–3 minutes.

3 Meanwhile, heat a wok or large frying pan until searing hot. Add about two tablespoons of the oil and swirl up the sides to heat through. Tip in the shallot with the garlic and ginger and stir-fry for 1 minute. Add the broccoli, courgette, carrot, peppers and finally the pak choi and continue to stir-fry for 2–3 minutes until all the vegetables are tender but still have a little bite.

4 Add the soy and oyster sauce to the vegetables and toss together briefly until just combined. Sprinkle over the sesame oil and spoon into Chinese-style bowls. Carve the rested pork into slices and arrange on top. Drizzle over any remaining sauce from the wok and serve at once.

55 Slow-roasted Pork with Fennel

JAMES MARTIN
MEAT

Serves 4

1 small pork shoulder, skin on

10 garlic cloves, peeled

100 g/4 oz fennel seeds

5–6 small dried red chillies, crumbled

juice of 5 lemons

3 tbsp olive oil

salt and freshly ground black pepper

basil pesto (from a jar is fine) and honey-roast carrots and parsnips (see introduction), to serve

Shoulder is one of the cheapest and tastiest cuts of pork. Cooked this way, the resulting sauce is full of flavour and the meat just falls off the bone. Honey-roast carrots and parsnips are easy to make. Simply preheat the oven to 200°C/400°F/Gas Mark 6 (fan oven 180°C from cold). Place even-sized batons of the vegetables in a large roasting tin and coat in olive oil, then drizzle over a little honey and season generously. Roast for 30–40 minutes until completely tender and slightly caramelized, shaking the tin occasionally to ensure even cooking.

1 Preheat the oven to 230°C/450°F/Gas Mark 8 (fan oven 210°C from cold). Using a small, sharp knife, score the skin of the pork shoulder with deep cuts about 0.5 cm/$\frac{1}{4}$ in apart. Place the garlic in a pestle and mortar with the fennel seeds, chilli to taste and some seasoning. Pound to a paste and then rub all over the scored pork shoulder, making sure that you get it right into the cuts on the skin.

2 Place the pork shoulder on a rack set over a roasting tin and roast for 30 minutes until the skin begins to crackle up, blister and brown. Remove from the oven, turn over and drizzle over half the lemon juice and two tablespoons of the olive oil.

3 Reduce the oven temperature to 120°C/225°F/Gas Mark $\frac{1}{4}$ (fan oven 100°C), and continue to roast the pork for at least another 8 hours – up to 24 hours is fine – turning occasionally and basting with a little of the remaining lemon juice and the olive oil. The pork shoulder is ready when the skin is crisp but the meat is completely soft. Test by pushing with your finger – the meat should give way and might even fall off the bone.

4 Transfer the pork to a carving board. Place the roasting tin directly on the hob and allow to bubble up. Tip in the remaining lemon juice and use to deglaze, scraping the bottom of the tin with a wooden spoon to remove any sediment. Remove the skin from the pork and cut into pieces, then carve the pork and arrange on plates with the crispy skin. Add a good dollop of pesto and some honey-roast carrots and parsnips to serve.

56 Aubergine and Mozzarella Stacks

JAMES MARTIN
VEGETARIAN

Serves 4

2 large aubergines

1 tbsp olive oil, plus extra for brushing

1 shallot, finely chopped

1 red chilli, seeded and finely chopped

4 garlic cloves, finely chopped

8 ripe plum tomatoes, peeled and chopped

good pinch of sugar

2 tbsp chopped fresh basil

25 g/1 oz fresh flat-leaf parsley leaves

1 tsp chopped fresh rosemary

grated rind of 1 lemon

4 buffalo mozzarella balls, each about 100 g/4 oz

salt and freshly ground black pepper

These Mediterranean stacks look impressive and yet are extremely easy to assemble. Each one should be four to five layers high – make sure you use the larger pieces for the bases and the smaller pieces on top. If it's the wrong time of year for decent plum tomatoes use a 400 g/14 oz can chopped tomatoes in rich tomato juice instead. And be sure to use buffalo mozzarella, not the one made from cow's milk, for maximum flavour.

1 Preheat the oven to 180°C/350°F/Gas Mark 4 (fan oven 160°C from cold). Heat a heavy-based griddle pan. Cut the aubergines into 1 cm/½ in slices, discarding the ends. Brush with olive oil and season lightly. Chargrill in batches on the heated griddle pan for 3 minutes on each side until softened and lightly charred. Transfer to a plate and leave to cool.

2 Meanwhile, make the sauce. Heat the tablespoon of olive oil in a frying pan. Add the shallot, chilli and one of the garlic cloves and sauté for about 5 minutes until the shallot is softened but not coloured. Add the chopped tomatoes, sugar and season to taste. Simmer for about 10 minutes until slightly reduced and thickened, stirring occasionally. Add the basil, remove from the heat and leave to cool.

3 To make the gremolata, finely chop the flat-leaf parsley and place in a bowl. Stir in the rosemary, lemon rind and remaining three garlic cloves. Cut the mozzarella into 1 cm/½ in slices. Place the four largest aubergine slices on an oiled baking sheet and sprinkle over a little of the gremolata, then season to taste. Continue to layer up the mozzarella with the remaining aubergine slices, adding a little of the gremolata and seasoning to each layer as you go. Make four even-sized stacks, finishing with a layer of aubergine. Bake for about 15 minutes or until the stacks are heated through and the mozzarella has begun to melt.

4 Transfer the cooled sauce to a food processor or liquidizer and blend to a purée. Return to a clean pan and just warm through. Arrange an aubergine and mozzarella stack in the centre of each plate and spoon around some of the warm sauce. Serve at once.

57 Artichokes Stuffed with Wild Mushrooms and Mascarpone

CELIA BROOKS BROWN
VEGETARIAN

Serves 4

2 tbsp white wine vinegar

2 tbsp olive oil

4 large globe artichokes

1 tbsp softened unsalted butter, plus extra for greasing

300 g/11 oz mixed wild mushrooms, cleaned and cut into small chunks (morels, chanterelles and ceps)

2 tsp fresh thyme leaves (or lemon thyme)

2 garlic cloves, finely chopped

75 ml/3 fl oz vermouth

175 g/6 oz mascarpone cheese

50 g/2 oz walnuts or pecan nuts, chopped

1–2 tbsp chopped fresh flat-leaf parsley

salt and freshly ground black pepper

lightly dressed green salad, to serve (optional)

Artichokes cannot be attacked with a knife and fork. Instead, each leaf has to be pulled away for eating and dipped in the wonderful creamy sauce. When all the leaves have gone the delicious heart can be enjoyed – talk about saving the best till last. Having the pan of acidulated water ready to drop the prepared artichokes into helps avoid the cut surfaces blackening.

1 Fill a large pan with water and add the vinegar, olive oil and a good pinch of salt. Meanwhile, trim the artichoke stalks close to the base and slice about a third off the top. Pull out what you can from the middle and then use a teaspoon to scoop out the hairy choke. As each artichoke is ready, place it in the pan of acidulated water. When they are all done, bring the pan to the boil and simmer for 30–40 minutes until the artichokes are tender or you can pull away a base leaf easily. Drain well and then place upside down on kitchen paper to dry off completely.

2 Preheat the oven to 220°C/425°F/Gas Mark 7 (fan oven 200°C from cold). To make the stuffing, heat a frying pan and add the butter. Once it has stopped foaming, add the mushrooms, thyme and garlic and season to taste. Sauté for a few minutes until the mushrooms have absorbed all the butter and are beginning to soften. Pour in the vermouth and cook, stirring, until almost all the liquid has evaporated. Add the mascarpone and allow to melt, stirring until well combined.

3 Arrange the artichokes in a greased baking dish and fill with the mushroom stuffing. Sprinkle over the walnuts or pecan nuts and bake for 15 minutes until heated through and golden on top. Arrange on plates with a little salad, if liked, and sprinkle over the parsley. Show guests how to use the leaves of the artichoke to scoop out the delicious, creamy filling.

58 Coconut Butternut Squash Stew

ANTONY WORRALL
THOMPSON VEGETARIAN

Serves 4–6

4 dried red chillies (5–7.5 cm/
2–3 in), seeded and chopped

6 spring onions, trimmed and
roughly chopped

2 large garlic cloves, chopped

2 lemongrass stalks, outer
leaves removed and remainder
chopped

2 tbsp groundnut oil, plus a little
extra if necessary

2 tsp ground coriander

$\frac{1}{2}$ tsp ground turmeric

1 tsp paprika

400 g/14 oz can coconut milk

150 ml/$\frac{1}{4}$ pint vegetable stock
or water

675 g/1$\frac{1}{2}$ lb butternut squash,
peeled, seeded and cut into
5 cm/2 in chunks

1 red pepper, seeded and cut
into julienne (matchsticks)

2 cardamom pods, crushed

1 cinnamon stick

1$\frac{1}{2}$ tbsp dark soy sauce

1$\frac{1}{2}$ tsp light muscovado sugar

1$\frac{1}{2}$ tsp freshly squeezed lemon
juice

salt and freshly ground black
pepper

handful of fresh coriander
leaves, to garnish

Thai fragrant rice, to serve

This strongly Thai-influenced dish is delicious for vegetarians and meat-eaters alike. It is quite a wet stew but can be thickened with cornflour slaked with a little water if required. Butternut squash is now readily available throughout the year and is far 'meatier' than pumpkin, not so fibrous and less watery, but it can be cooked in exactly the same way. Choose ones that are shiny and firm and feel heavy for their size.

1 Place the chillies in a heatproof bowl and pour over enough warm water to cover. Set aside for 10 minutes to soften, then drain and place in a food processor or liquidizer. Add the spring onions, garlic and lemongrass and then blend to a paste, adding a little oil through the feeder tube if necessary.

2 Heat the two tablespoons of groundnut oil in a heavy-based pan over a medium-low heat. Add the chilli paste and cook, stirring for a few minutes, until it is fragrant and no longer tastes raw. Add the ground coriander, turmeric and paprika and continue to stir for 1 minute. Pour in the coconut milk and simmer for 5 minutes, stirring continuously.

3 Stir the stock into the pan and bring to a simmer. Reduce the heat to low and add the butternut squash, red pepper, cardamom and cinnamon stick, and season to taste. Simmer, partially covered, for 20–25 minutes until the butternut squash is completely tender and the sauce is reduced and thickened.

4 Stir the soy sauce into the pan with the sugar and lemon juice and simmer for another 2 minutes. Ladle the stew into bowls and garnish with the coriander leaves. Serve at once with Thai fragrant rice.

59 Risotto with Lettuce and Spring Onions

VALENTINA HARRIS
VEGETARIAN

Serves 4

about 2 litres/3½ pints vegetable stock

40 g/1½ oz unsalted butter

8 spring onions, finely chopped

350 g/12 oz arborio (risotto) rice

120 ml/4 fl oz white wine (1 small glass)

1 round lettuce, coarsely shredded

4 tbsp freshly grated Parmesan

salt and freshly ground black pepper

The key to the success of this risotto is buying top-quality ingredients. Arborio rice is now readily available. It takes its name from the little town in the Vercelli region where it was first developed in 1946. It can absorb a great deal of liquid and benefits from being rested once it is almost cooked. The Italians call this process *mantecare*.

1 Heat a large heavy-based sauté pan. Place the stock in a separate pan and bring to a gentle simmer. Add half the butter to the sauté pan and, once it has stopped foaming, tip in the spring onions. Cook gently for a few minutes until softened, then stir in the rice and toast the grains quickly but thoroughly – for about 3 minutes.

2 When the rice is crackling dry, pour in the wine and stir, evaporating it. Add three ladlefuls of stock to completely submerge the rice. Stir thoroughly, and allow the liquid to be absorbed, then lower the heat and continue to add stock a ladleful or two at a time, stirring constantly between each addition. The rice itself will let you know when it needs more liquid by allowing a clear trail to open up behind the spoon as you draw it across the pan.

3 After about 20 minutes, the rice should have swollen and become creamy, and the grains should still be chewy, but not chalky. In no way should there be a hint of rice pudding about it. Remove from the heat, stir in the lettuce and continue to stir until the leaves have wilted, then add the remaining butter, season to taste and stir in the Parmesan. Cover with a lid or plate and leave to rest for about 4 minutes, then transfer to plates and eat at once.

60 Chickpea Fritters

ANTONY WORRALL
THOMPSON
VEGETARIAN

Serves 4

1 litre/1³/₄ pints water

250 g/9 oz gram flour

1 tbsp finely chopped fresh
flat-leaf parsley

olive oil, for frying

75 g/3 oz polenta or semolina

salt and freshly ground black
pepper

mixed salad, to serve

This recipe uses gram (chickpea) flour, which is available from super-markets, and you'll also find it in most health-food shops and ethnic stores. I like the fritters stuffed into split warm pitta bread with shredded lettuce, slivers of red onion and chopped-up cucumber and tomatoes. Drizzle over a little tzatziki just before serving and watch them disappear.

1 Pour the water into a large pan and almost bring to the boil. Remove from the heat and gradually add the gram flour, mixing it very well to help prevent lumps forming. Return to the heat and cook gently for 30 minutes until smooth and thickened, beating occasionally with a wooden spoon.

2 Stir the parsley into the chickpea mixture and season to taste. Pour on to a wet marble surface or non-stick baking sheet and flatten with a spatula to a 1 cm/¹/₂ in thickness. Level the top with the back of a wooden spoon, cover with cling film and chill for at least 1 hour – overnight is best – to firm it up.

3 Heat 1 cm/¹/₂ in of oil in a sauté pan. Using a sharp knife, cut the chickpea mixture into 7.5 cm/3 in squares or stamp out rounds with a pastry cutter. Roll in the polenta or semolina to coat. Shallow-fry the fritters for 2–3 minutes on each side until crisp and golden brown. Drain on kitchen paper. Arrange on a large platter and serve at once with salad.

61 Foolproof Cheese Soufflé

ROSA BADEN POWELL
VEGETARIAN

Serves 2

150 ml/¼ pint milk

25 g/1 oz unsalted butter, plus extra for greasing

25 g/1 oz plain flour (Italian 00 flour if possible)

1 tsp Dijon mustard

2 egg yolks

75 g/3 oz Gruyère cheese, finely grated

4 egg whites

pinch of cayenne pepper

salt and freshly ground black pepper

lightly dressed mixed salad and crusty French bread, to serve (optional)

I have made this recipe a thousand times and it always works so please don't be afraid to give it a go. The art of making a good soufflé is in how you beat your egg whites. If they are not at the right soft-peak stage then the soufflé will not rise to its full potential.
I normally clean the beaters of my electric mixer with lemon juice to make sure that there is no greasy residue left on them, which would prevent the egg whites from reaching the right consistency.

1 Preheat the oven to 200°C/400°F/Gas Mark 6 (fan oven 180°C from cold). Heat the milk in a pan until just below boiling point. Meanwhile, melt the butter in a separate pan, stir in the flour and cook for 1 minute. Remove from the heat and gradually add the milk, a little at a time, beating until smooth after each addition. Bring to the boil, then reduce the heat and simmer for 1 minute until thickened and smooth, stirring occasionally. Remove from the heat. Season generously and stir in the mustard. Leave to cool for 1 minute while you butter two individual soufflé dishes (or one large dish).

2 Beat the yolks one at a time into the sauce and then beat in most of the Gruyère cheese, reserving a little to garnish. Whisk the egg whites in a separate bowl with an electric mixer until you have soft peaks – be careful not to overdo. Fold into the Gruyère sauce and use to fill the prepared soufflé dishes three-quarters full. Run a finger around the top to help the soufflé rise out of the dishes and get the top-hat effect. Sprinkle the remaining Gruyère on top with the cayenne and bake for 15–17 minutes until well risen and lightly golden. Serve immediately straight on to the table with a bowl of salad and a basket of bread, if liked.

62 Lentil and Sprout Curry

RESHMA MARTIN
VEGETARIAN

Serves 2

100 g/4 oz split yellow lentils (*moong*)

1 tbsp olive oil

1 tsp cumin seeds

2 garlic cloves, crushed

5 cm/2 in piece of fresh root ginger, peeled and finely chopped

2 green chillies, seeded and finely chopped

$^1/_2$ tsp ground turmeric

400 ml/14 fl oz warm water

150 g/5 oz Brussels sprouts, trimmed and quartered, or halved if small

150 g/5 oz Brussels sprout tops, shredded

1 ripe tomato, seeded and finely diced

handful of chopped fresh coriander

salt and freshly ground black pepper

cooked basmati rice, to serve

This recipe shows how to spice up ordinary winter greens into a tasty Gujarati vegetarian curry. I always put my lentils to soak in the morning before going to work and then I can have dinner on the table in 15 minutes that evening. I've used *moong* lentils, which are available from most supermarkets. They are fairly small lentils that come from the split green seed of the bean sprout.

1 Place the lentils in a heatproof bowl and cover with boiling water. Set aside to soak for at least 4 hours (up to 8 hours is best). Tip the soaked lentils into a sieve and rinse well under warm water; leave to drain.

2 Heat the olive oil a large heavy-based pan with a lid, add the cumin seeds and stir-fry for 30 seconds to 1 minute until lightly browned. Remove the pan from the heat and add the garlic, ginger and chillies, stirring to combine. Return to the heat and stir-fry for another 30 seconds or so, being very careful not to let it burn.

3 Add the drained lentils to the pan with the turmeric, 300 ml/$^1/_2$ pint of the warm water and half a teaspoon of salt. Bring to the boil, cover and simmer gently for 10 minutes until the lentils are tender. Be careful not to allow the liquid to reduce by more than a third; if it does, add a little extra. To check that the lentils are tender, scoop a few out with a spoon and try crushing them gently between your fingers.

4 Add the Brussels sprouts and tops to the pan with the remaining 100 ml/ $3^1/_2$ fl oz of warm water. Stir until well combined and season to taste, then simmer for another 5 minutes until the Brussels sprouts are just tender but still have a little bite to them, stirring occasionally. Season to taste. Spoon the curry on to plates with some basmati rice. Scatter over the tomato and coriander and serve at once.

63 Tomato and Goats' Cheese Galette with Spinach

ED BAINES
VEGETARIAN

Serves 2–4

200 g/7 oz ready-rolled puff pastry sheet, thawed if frozen

a little plain flour, for dusting

a little unsalted butter, for greasing

675 g/1½ lb tender young spinach leaves

1 egg yolk, lightly beaten

4 firm ripe tomatoes, thinly sliced

150 g/5 oz soft Welsh goats' cheese, rolled in herbs

olive oil, for drizzling

1 tsp dried thyme

salt and freshly ground black pepper

lightly dressed rocket salad, to serve (optional)

This is one of my favourite tarts. The sweetness of the tomatoes complements the saltiness of the goats' cheese perfectly. It is good served hot or cold and makes an excellent vegetarian option. Alternatively, cut into small wedges and serve as part of antipasti platter with Parma ham, roasted peppers and semi-sun-dried tomatoes. It also makes great picnic food as it is so easy to transport – the possibilities are endless.

1 Roll out the pastry on a lightly floured board until it is 2 cm/¾ in thick and then cut out a 30 cm/12 in round, using a plate as a template. Transfer to a buttered baking sheet, then chill for at least 30 minutes.

2 Meanwhile, preheat the oven to 190°C/375°F/Gas Mark 5 (fan oven 170°C from cold). Steam the spinach for 2–3 minutes until wilted and cooked through. Leave to cool, then squeeze out all the excess moisture with kitchen paper and roughly chop.

3 Brush the chilled pastry round with the egg yolk and arrange the spinach on top, leaving a 1 cm/½ in gap around the edge as a border. Arrange the tomatoes on top in an overlapping layer and scatter the goats' cheese on top of that.

4 Drizzle a little olive oil over the tart and sprinkle on the thyme. Season to taste and bake for 15–20 minutes until the tart is cooked through, puffed up and golden. Cut into slices and arrange on plates with some rocket salad, if liked.

65 Asparagus Tarts

ANTONY WORRALL
THOMPSON
VEGETARIAN

Serves 4

**500 g/1 lb 2 oz ready-made
puff pastry, thawed if frozen**

a little plain flour, for dusting

unsalted butter, for greasing

3–4 tbsp extra virgin olive oil

1 large onion, thinly sliced

16 asparagus spears, trimmed

1 egg, beaten

2 tbsp freshly grated Parmesan

**salt and freshly ground black
pepper**

tomato salad, to serve (optional)

These tarts make good use of a small amount of asparagus, while roasting gives it a completely different texture and flavour. To trim the asparagus, chop every stem to where it starts to feel woody and, unless they are particularly fresh, peel the lowest 3–5 cm/1–2 in just to be safe.

1 Roll out the pastry on a lightly floured board to a 0.5 cm/¼ in thickness. Cut the pastry into four even-sized rectangles, each about 20 cm/8 in x 10 cm/4 in, and trim down the edges. Arrange on large greased baking sheets, prick all over with a fork and chill for at least 30 minutes.

2 Meanwhile, preheat the oven to 200°C/400°F/Gas Mark 6 (fan oven 180°C from cold). Heat two tablespoons of the olive oil in a frying pan and cook the onion for 3–4 minutes until softened but not coloured, stirring occasionally. Remove from the heat and set aside to cool.

3 Blanch the asparagus in a pan of boiling water for 1 minute. Drain and refresh quickly under cold running water. Set aside to cool completely.

4 Spread the softened onion over the pastry bases, leaving a 1 cm/½ in border around the edges. Arrange the asparagus spears over the onion and brush lightly with the remaining olive oil.

5 Brush the pastry borders with the beaten egg and sprinkle over the Parmesan. Season to taste and bake for 15–20 minutes or until the pastry is puffed up and golden brown. Remove the tarts from the oven, transfer to plates and serve hot or warm, with the tomato salad, if liked.

65 Polenta Gnocchi with Chilli and Roasted Pepper Sauce

GENNARO CONTALDO
VEGETARIAN

Serves 4

1 red and 1 yellow pepper

3 tbsp olive oil

1 garlic clove, squashed but left whole

1 small red chilli

50 ml/2 fl oz white wine

50 ml/2 fl oz vegetable stock

25 g/1 oz unsalted butter

125 g/4½ oz quick-cook polenta

25 g/1 oz fontina cheese, diced

25 g/1 oz freshly grated Parmesan

salt and freshly ground black pepper

This recipe uses quick-cook polenta (*polenta svelte*), which is ready in a few minutes. It doesn't have quite the same taste as traditional polenta but it makes a very acceptable substitute if you don't want to stand over the stove for ages. For a non-vegetarian alternative, add two anchovy fillets to the sauce: cook before adding the garlic to the olive oil, stirring over a low heat for a few minutes until they have almost dissolved into the oil.

1 First make the sauce. Preheat the grill. Arrange the red and yellow peppers on a grill rack and toast for 20–30 minutes until well charred and blistered, turning regularly. Transfer to a polythene bag and secure with a knot. Leave the peppers to cool completely, then peel. Slice the flesh into thin strips, discarding the seeds and cores. Place in a bowl and set aside until needed.

2 Heat the olive oil in a large pan. Add the garlic and chilli and cook for a minute or two until the garlic becomes golden brown, then remove and discard the garlic and chilli. Add the roasted pepper strips and sauté for a few minutes. Pour in the wine and let it bubble until it evaporates slightly, then add the stock and simmer for 5 minutes. Season to taste. Remove from the heat and set aside.

3 To make the polenta gnocchi, place 500 ml/18 fl oz of water in a large pan with two teaspoons of salt and the butter. Bring to the boil, stirring continuously until the butter melts. Reduce the heat and gradually add the polenta in a thin continuous stream, stirring constantly with a wooden spoon. Cook according to packet instructions until you have achieved a medium-thick consistency. Beat in the fontina and Parmesan and remove from the heat.

4 Make quenelles with the polenta mixture by taking a tablespoon of it, scooping it off the spoon with another tablespoon and then scooping it back again until it is a neat oval shape, turning the spoons against each other. Have a bowl of cold water ready by your side so that the tablespoons can be dipped in water after each quenelle is made – this makes it easier for the quenelle to slide off the spoon. Put the pepper sauce back on a moderate heat. Add the polenta gnocchi and allow to warm through. Transfer the polenta gnocchi on to plates and spoon over the sauce. Serve at once.

66 Warm Salad of Asparagus, Field Mushrooms and Fresh Peas

ANTONY WORRALL
THOMPSON
ACCOMPANIMENTS

Serves 4

20 asparagus spears, trimmed and peeled

175 g/6 oz shelled new-season peas

4 tbsp extra virgin olive oil

1 garlic clove, crushed

8 small field mushrooms, peeled, stalks removed

1 ciabatta loaf, split open and then cut in half again cross-ways

1 shallot, finely chopped

3 tbsp dry Martini

50 g/2 oz unsalted butter, cubed and chilled

1 tbsp chopped fresh flat-leaf parsley

1 tbsp snipped fresh chives

1 tsp chopped fresh tarragon

1 tbsp freshly squeezed lemon juice

25 g/1 oz each rocket and watercress leaves

salt and freshly ground black pepper

Warm salads were all the rage during the nouvelle eighties, more often than not weird-and-not-so-wonderful combinations. This one was made to last: fresh and vibrant with clean flavours. Perfect as an accompaniment to a simple piece of grilled fish or lamb, it would also, of course, make a very nice starter or light lunch served on its own. If you can't get hold of new-season peas, frozen petits pois are a good year-round alternative.

1 Cook the asparagus in a pan of boiling salted water for 1 minute, then remove with a slotted spoon and quickly refresh in a bowl of iced water. Set aside. Add the peas to the asparagus cooking water and cook for 2–5 minutes, depending on how small the peas are; drain and set aside.

2 Heat a griddle pan until smoking hot. Combine the olive oil and garlic in a small bowl and brush over the asparagus and both sides of the mushrooms, reserving some to use later. Season generously and arrange the mushrooms on the pan. Griddle on one side for 4 minutes, then turn over, add the asparagus and cook for another 4 minutes, turning the asparagus spears once. Keep warm. Brush the pieces of ciabatta on both sides with some of the remaining garlic oil and griddle for a minute or two until both sides are toasted.

3 Place the remaining garlic oil in a small pan – you should have at least one tablespoon in total. Add the shallot and cook gently for a few minutes until softened but not coloured, stirring occasionally. Add the Martini, increase the heat and cook for another minute. Remove from the heat and whisk in the butter a little at a time. Fold in the blanched peas with the parsley, chives, tarragon and lemon juice. Season to taste. Return to a gentle heat and allow to just warm through.

4 Combine the rocket and watercress and divide among plates and then top each one with a piece of griddled ciabatta. Arrange the mushrooms and asparagus on top and spoon over the peas and buttery juices to serve.

67 Baked Herby Tomatoes

ANTONY WORRALL
THOMPSON
ACCOMPANIMENTS

Serves 4

450 g/1 lb large tomatoes (ripe but firm)

1 shallot, finely diced

2 garlic cloves, finely chopped

1 tsp fresh thyme leaves

2 tbsp extra virgin olive oil

4 canned anchovies, finely chopped

2 tbsp roughly chopped fresh flat-leaf parsley

$1/2$ tsp dried chilli flakes

50 g/2 oz fresh white breadcrumbs

salt and freshly ground black pepper

extra virgin olive oil and balsamic vinegar, to garnish

I love these for breakfast with good-quality crispy bacon and creamy scrambled eggs. They also make good partners to grilled or roast meats. Thankfully it is now much easier to find tomatoes that have been specially grown for flavour (what were they grown for before? It makes you wonder…). Choose well-ripened specimens or try leaving them in the kitchen window for a couple of days – that normally does the trick.

1 Cut the tomatoes in half horizontally and carefully remove the seeds. Sprinkle the cut sides with salt and place cut-side down on kitchen paper to draw out some of the liquid. Leave to stand for 20 minutes.

2 Preheat the oven to 200°C/400°F/Gas Mark 6 (fan oven 180°C from cold). Place the shallot in a food processor with the garlic, thyme, oil and anchovies and then blend to a smooth paste. Transfer to a bowl and fold in the parsley, chilli flakes and breadcrumbs until well combined. Season to taste.

3 Spoon the bread mixture into the tomato cavities and bake for about 15 minutes until bubbling and golden. Transfer to a dish and serve hot or at room temperature drizzled with extra virgin olive oil and balsamic vinegar.

68 Stuffed Baby Peppers

GENNARO CONTALDO
ACCOMPANIMENTS

Serves 4

2 large potatoes, cut into chunks

8 red or yellow baby peppers

75 g/3 oz provolone cheese, diced

4 tbsp freshly grated Parmesan

1 egg, beaten

3 tbsp snipped fresh chives

a little olive oil, for drizzling

salt and freshly ground black pepper

If you have trouble getting hold of baby peppers, try using the small, sweet, long peppers that just need to be slit lengthways to remove the seeds. Make the filling as described below but cut the provolone cheese into strips and place over the top of the peppers. They will need only 20 minutes in the oven. If you can't find either type of pepper use ordinary peppers and serve one per person. They will need 40–45 minutes' cooking, depending on their size.

1 Preheat the oven to 200°C/400°F/Gas Mark 6 (fan oven 180°C from cold). Place the potatoes in a pan of boiling salted water, then cover and simmer for 20–25 minutes or until tender. Drain and mash until smooth. Transfer to a bowl and set aside to cool.

2 Carefully remove the stalks from the peppers and set aside. With a small sharp knife, remove the white membrane and seeds from inside the peppers, taking care not to tear the flesh.

3 Add the provolone cheese to the mashed potatoes with the Parmesan, egg and chives. Season to taste and mix until well combined. Using a teaspoon, fill the peppers three-quarters full with the potato mixture and then put the stalks back in place, like a stopper.

4 Pack the peppers tightly into an ovenproof dish and drizzle with olive oil. Bake for about 30 minutes until completely tender but still holding their shape. Transfer the dish straight to the table and serve at once; they are also delicious eaten cold.

69 French Bean Salad with Mint

ANTONY WORRALL
THOMPSON
ACCOMPANIMENTS

Serves 4

350 g/12 oz French beans, topped

3 fresh mint sprigs

1 garlic clove, peeled

4 tbsp extra virgin olive oil

juice of 1 lemon

salt and freshly ground black pepper

Lightly cooked French beans make wonderful salads – only be careful not to add the lemon juice until just before serving as the beans will lose their vibrant green colour. Contrary to popular belief, French beans (*haricots verts*) don't need tailing, only topping; the tails are perfectly edible. Alternatively, try using runner beans that have been topped and tailed then sliced.

1 Cook the beans in a pan of boiling salted water until tender. Drain and quickly refresh under cold running water.

2 Finely chop the mint and garlic by hand with a sharp knife or in a mini blender. Transfer to a large bowl and mix in the olive oil and lemon juice until well combined. Season to taste. Fold in the blanched beans until evenly coated. Serve warm or cold.

70 Green Beans with Ginger and Mustard Seeds

MANJU MALHI
ACCOMPANIMENTS

Serves 2

1 tbsp olive oil

$\frac{1}{2}$ tsp black mustard seeds

200 g/7 oz green beans, trimmed and cut into 5 cm/2 in pieces

1 tsp cumin powder

1 tsp freshly grated root ginger

$\frac{1}{2}$ tsp salt

Indian tradition has it that a mixture made from ginger (an aphrodisiac), honey and egg taken at night for a month is a remedy for impotence. I can't make the same claim for this dish, but it doesn't need much effort to cook and will impress any discriminating vegetarian or make a wonderful accompaniment.

1 Heat the olive oil in a pan, and then add the mustard seeds. A few seconds later, tip in the beans with the cumin and sauté for 1 minute.

2 Stir the ginger into the pan with the salt, and sauté over a low heat for 5 minutes or until the beans are completely tender. Transfer to a serving dish and serve at once.

71 Spicy Stir-fried Mushrooms

KEN HOM
ACCOMPANIMENTS

Serves 4

1 tbsp groundnut oil

2 garlic cloves, finely chopped

knob of fresh root ginger, peeled and finely chopped (about 2 tsp in total)

2 spring onions, finely chopped

450 g/1 lb small button mushrooms, trimmed

2 tsp sweet chilli sauce or chilli bean sauce

1 tbsp Shaoxing rice wine or dry sherry

1 tbsp chicken or vegetable stock

2 tsp caster sugar

1 tsp salt

$\frac{1}{2}$ tsp freshly ground black pepper

2 tsp toasted sesame oil

Although button mushrooms are common in Europe and America, they were almost unknown in China until quite recently. They are now increasingly popular there as their mild, subtle flavour makes them perfect for stir-frying with Chinese spices. This dish is simple to make and reheats well. Serve as part of a large banquet-style meal, or, as I like to, on its own with plain steamed rice.

1 Heat a wok or large frying pan until smoking hot. Add the oil, swirl up the sides and when it is very hot and slightly smoking, tip in the garlic, ginger and spring onions. Stir-fry for 20 seconds.

2 Add the mushrooms to the wok and stir-fry for another 30 seconds. Add the chilli sauce, rice wine or sherry, stock, sugar, salt and pepper and continue to stir-fry for about 5 minutes or until the mushrooms are cooked through and have absorbed all the spices and seasonings.

3 Just before serving, sprinkle over the sesame oil and give the mixture a couple of quick stirs. Transfer to a serving dish and serve at once, as the mushrooms are particularly delicious when hot.

72 Creamy Broad Beans

ANTONY WORRALL
THOMPSON
ACCOMPANIMENTS

Serves 4

450 g/1 lb fresh or frozen broad beans

5 tbsp chicken or vegetable stock

pinch of caster sugar

2 tbsp chopped mixed herbs, such as chives, chervil and summer savory

1 egg yolk

150 ml/¼ pint double cream

salt and freshly ground black pepper

Broad beans are one of the first vegetables of spring, appearing in the shops in mid-May or early June. For me, few things taste better than a dish of fresh new season broad beans drizzled with melted butter. This recipe is great served with grilled bacon and floury new potatoes, but would work well with most meats or fish. It may seem like a bore to slip the beans out of their white papery skins once they have been cooked but it is absolutely worth the effort – I promise.

1 Cook the broad beans in a pan of boiling salted water for 1–2 minutes until just tender. Drain and quickly refresh under cold running water, then pop the beans out of their skins.

2 Place the skinned beans in a pan with the stock, sugar and herbs. Season to taste and bring to a simmer, then continue to cook until almost all the liquid has evaporated.

3 Beat the egg yolk in a small bowl with the cream, then add to the beans and just warm through until the cream has slightly thickened. Do not re-boil. Transfer to a warmed serving dish and serve at once.

73 Garlic Potatoes

ANTONY WORRALL
THOMPSON
ACCOMPANIMENTS

Serves 4

sunflower or vegetable oil, for deep-frying

450 g/1 lb tiny new potatoes, scrubbed

50 g/2 oz freshly grated Parmesan

50 g/2 oz fresh white fine breadcrumbs

2 eggs, beaten

100 g/4 oz unsalted butter

4 garlic cloves, finely chopped

1 tsp chopped fresh flat-leaf parsley

salt and freshly ground black pepper

This is certainly not the recipe for someone who is watching what they eat, but you know what they say – a little in moderation … Tiny new potatoes are the first of the season, plucked out of the ground before they're fully grown. The paper-thin skin may be red or white and most have quite a waxy texture.

1 Heat a deep-fat fryer or a deep-sided pan half filled with oil to 180°C/350°F. Cook the potatoes in a pan of boiling salted water for 8–10 minutes or until just tender.

2 Place the Parmesan and breadcrumbs in a shallow dish and place the beaten eggs in a shallow bowl. Season to taste.

3 Drain the potatoes and leave until they are just cool enough to handle but still hot. Roll in the breadcrumb mixture and then dip in the beaten egg. Finally roll in the breadcrumb mixture again until well coated.

4 Deep-fry the potatoes for 5–6 minutes until crisp and golden. Meanwhile, melt the butter in a small frying pan and cook the garlic for a couple of minutes until golden. Remove from the heat, season to taste and stir in the parsley. Drain the potatoes on kitchen paper and transfer to a warm serving dish. Drizzle over the garlic butter and serve at once.

74 Baby Potatoes with Fennel

MANJU MALHI
ACCOMPANIMENTS

Serves 2

300 g/11 oz baby salad potatoes

3 tbsp vegetable oil

½ tsp fennel seeds

½ tsp salt

pinch of garam masala

½ tsp chilli powder

When I first made this dish, I couldn't believe how easy it was to prepare – I still make it when I'm bored with mashed potato. 'Garam masala' means 'the warming spices' and is normally a mixture of toasted cinnamon, black pepper, whole cloves, cumin seeds, mace, cardamom seeds and bay leaves, which are toasted before being ground down to a powder. It actually improves daily for the first few weeks after grinding, but then starts to lose its potency, so don't be tempted to make too much at once. Of course, there are a number of ready-made alternatives but none will be as good as the one you make yourself.

1 Cook the potatoes in a pan of boiling salted water for 7–8 minutes, then drain and leave to cool.

2 Heat the oil in a frying pan, add the fennel seeds, salt, garam masala and chilli powder and cook for 1 minute, stirring.

3 Tip the cooled potatoes into the pan and sauté for another 3–4 minutes until golden brown and heated through. Transfer to a serving dish and serve at once.

75 Sweet Potato Gratin

CURTIS STONE
ACCOMPANIMENTS

Serves 4

6 small sweet potatoes (preferably orange-fleshed)

knob of unsalted butter

250 g/9 oz mature Cheddar, gratcd

500 ml/18 fl oz double cream

salt and freshly ground black pepper

This has to be one of my favourite accompaniments at the restaurant, where I often serve it with beef or lamb. One of its great advantages is that it can be made in advance and reheated in individual portions on a baking sheet. It also keeps well in a cool oven. I normally use a 6 cm/2½ in straight-sided cooking ring as a cutter, which creates perfect little layered sweet-potato towers every time.

1 Preheat the oven to 180°C/350°F/Gas Mark 4 (fan oven 160°C from cold). Peel the sweet potatoes and thinly slice using a mandolin cutter or very sharp knife, being very careful of your fingers.

2 Generously butter a shallow gratin dish and layer up the sweet potato slices and Cheddar, seasoning as you go. Pour over the cream and finish with a layer of the Cheddar. Cover with foil and bake for 15 minutes, then remove the foil and cook for another 10 minutes until completely tender and nicely browned.

3 Stamp out 2 x 10 cm/4 in rounds with a straight-sided cutter and transfer to a non-stick baking sheet with a fish slice (the leftovers can be used at another time). Arrange on plates and serve immediately.

104

76 Baked Chocolate Mousse with Passion Fruit Cream

JAMES MARTIN
DESSERTS

Serves 6–8

150 g/5 oz unsalted butter, plus extra for greasing

300 g/11 oz plain chocolate (at least 70 per cent cocoa solids)

6 eggs

50 g/2 oz caster sugar

FOR THE PASSION FRUIT CREAM:

3 passion fruit

250 g/9 oz mascarpone cheese

50 ml/2 fl oz double cream

3 tbsp sifted icing sugar, plus extra for dusting

a little cocoa powder, for dusting

fresh mint sprigs, to decorate

The beauty of this dessert is that it is smooth, silky and rich. It's ideal for a dinner party as you can make everything the day before and keep it in the fridge until needed. I also like this served with crisp, wafer-thin biscuits. The recipe for passion fruit cream works with just about any fruit that can be puréed.

1 Preheat the oven to 180°C/350°F/Gas Mark 4 (fan oven 160°C from cold). Butter a 20 cm/8 in loose-bottomed cake tin and set aside. Melt the butter and chocolate in a heatproof bowl set over a pan of simmering water. Remove from the heat and leave to cool.

2 Separate the eggs and place the whites and yolks in separate large bowls. Whisk the egg whites with an electric mixer until stiff peaks have formed.

3 Add the caster sugar to the egg yolks and whisk with an electric mixer until pale and thickened. Whisk in the cooled chocolate mixture, then fold in the egg whites. Pour into the cake tin and bake for about 20 minutes until just set and firm to the touch but still with a slight wobble in the middle. Leave to cool.

4 To make the passion fruit cream, cut the passion fruit in half and scoop out the seeds and pulp into a bowl. Add the mascarpone, cream and icing sugar and beat with an electric mixer until smooth. Cover with cling film and chill until needed.

5 Take large spoonfuls of the chocolate mousse and arrange on plates. Dust with icing sugar and cocoa powder and add a quenelle of passion fruit cream. Decorate with the mint sprigs to serve.

77 Warm Chocolate Sponge with Chocolate Sauce and Chantilly Cream

TONY TOBIN
DESSERTS

Serves 8

600 ml/1 pint double cream, well chilled

1 tbsp caster sugar

150 g/5 oz plain chocolate, broken into pieces

FOR THE SPONGE PUDDINGS:

unsalted butter, for greasing

100 g/4 oz caster sugar, plus extra for dusting

100 g/4 oz plain chocolate, broken into pieces

finely grated rind of 1 orange

6 eggs

100 g/4 oz ground almonds

50 g/2 oz ready-made chocolate cake, broken into crumbs

I had this pudding at a restaurant in Sussex and liked it so much that I ordered a second helping. The German chef who made it came out to meet me and very kindly gave me the recipe, which he considered his *pièce de résistance*. The sponges are perfect served with a warm chocolate sauce spooned on top and a very cold Chantilly cream.

1 Preheat the oven to 180°C/350°F/Gas Mark 4 (fan oven 160°C from cold). To make the sponge puddings, generously butter 8 x 120 ml/4 fl oz metal dariole moulds and then lightly dust each one with caster sugar.

2 Place the chocolate in a heatproof bowl with the orange rind and set over a pan of simmering water. Allow to melt, then remove from the heat and leave to cool a little.

3 Separate the eggs and place in different bowls. Add the sugar to the egg yolks and whisk with an electric mixer until pale and thickened. Fold in the cooled melted chocolate followed by the ground almonds and the cake crumbs.

4 Whisk the egg whites with an electric mixer until stiff peaks have formed and gently fold into the chocolate mixture until just combined. Spoon into the prepared moulds and place in a bain marie (large roasting tin half filled with boiling water). Cover each pudding with a buttered circle of foil and bake for 20 minutes until well risen and just firm to the touch.

5 Meanwhile, prepare the chantilly cream. Place half the cream in a bowl with the tablespoon of sugar and whisk until soft peaks have formed – be careful not to overdo it. Cover with cling film and chill until needed. Place the rest of the cream in a small pan with the chocolate and cook over a gentle heat until the chocolate has melted and a smooth, shiny sauce has formed. Keep warm.

6 Carefully unmould the puddings on to plates and spoon a little of the chocolate sauce over each one. Add a spoonful of the Chantilly cream to the side of each one and serve at once.

78 Roast Pineapple Galette with a Ginger Nut Crumble Topping

JEANNE RANKIN
DESSERTS

Serves 4

200 g/7 oz ready-rolled puff pastry, thawed if frozen

a little plain flour, for dusting

1 large ripe pineapple, peeled and cored

FOR THE TOPPING:

150 g/5 oz almonds or hazelnuts, toasted and roughly chopped

150 g/5 oz ginger nut biscuits, crumbled

50 g/2 oz sugar

pared rind of $\frac{1}{2}$ lemon, very finely chopped

75 g/3oz unsalted butter, diced and chilled

crème fraîche, whipped cream or vanilla ice cream, to serve

I just love this French-style galette, which was inspired by the time I spent with the Roux brothers as a pastry chef. The secret is to keep the pastry base very thin and not be tempted to load on the toppings – the right balance is crucial. Banana or mango also have a particular affinity with the ginger nut topping and would make a good alternative to pineapple.

1 Preheat the oven to 190°C/375°F/Gas Mark 5 (fan oven 170°C from cold). Place the pastry on a lightly floured board and roll it out as thinly as possible, then cut out four rounds, each about 12 cm/4 $\frac{1}{2}$ in in diameter. Transfer the pastry rounds on to baking sheets, and prick all over with a fork. Bake for 10–12 minutes until golden brown and the pastry looks flaky. Remove from oven and set aside to cool.

2 To make the topping, place the almonds or hazelnuts in a large bowl with the crumbled biscuits, sugar and lemon rind. Add the butter and work with your fingertips until it is well blended, but do not allow the butter to melt too much or you will end up with a paste.

3 Slice the pineapple into very thin rounds, about 0.5 cm/$\frac{1}{4}$ in thick. Arrange in a slightly overlapping layer on the cooled pastry rounds. Sprinkle over the ginger nut topping to cover completely and bake for another 10–12 minutes or until the topping is crisp and lightly golden and the pineapple can be pierced easily with a fork. Remove from oven, and allow to cool slightly. To serve, arrange the galettes on plates and add a dollop of crème fraîche, whipped cream or vanilla ice cream.

79 Meringue Roulade with Raspberries and Lemon Syllabub Filling

THANE PRINCE
DESSERTS

Serves 6–8

a little butter, for greasing

4 large egg whites

225 g/8 oz caster sugar

50 g/2 oz shredded coconut or flaked almonds

100 g/4 oz raspberries

FOR THE SYLLABUB:

5 tbsp clear honey

grated rind and juice of 2 lemons

grated rind and juice of 1 orange

600 ml/1 pint double cream

2 tbsp brandy or sherry (optional)

This meringue roulade with its lemon syllabub filling is perfectly decadent, especially if you add a hint of alcohol. For such a simple dessert, it really does impress, and you can have it prepared well in advance with no last-minute worries. The fresh raspberries cut through the richness of the meringue and creamy syllabub.

1 Preheat the oven to 200°C/400°F/Gas Mark 6 (fan oven 180°C from cold). To make the roulade, lightly grease a Swiss roll tin and line with non-stick baking parchment. Place the egg whites in a spotlessly clean bowl and whisk until very stiff. This is best done with a freestanding electric mixer, but a balloon whisk or ordinary electric mixer is also fine.

2 Now add the sugar one third at a time, whisking well after each addition. Once all the sugar has been added continue to whisk until the mixture is very thick and glossy. Spread over the prepared Swiss roll tin and then sprinkle with the coconut or almonds. Bake for 15–20 minutes until golden brown and just firm to the touch.

3 Meanwhile, make the syllabub. Place the honey in a large bowl and stir in the lemon and orange rinds and juice until the honey has completely dissolved. Add the cream with the brandy or sherry, if using, and whisk until floppy soft peaks have formed. Cover with cling film and chill until needed.

4 Remove the cooked roulade from the oven and immediately turn out on to a piece of non-stick baking parchment or a clean tea towel. Leave to cool for 15 minutes and then carefully peel off the baking parchment. When the roulade is completely cold, spread over the syllabub and scatter the raspberries on top. Carefully roll up and transfer to a plate, seam-side down. Cover loosely with foil and chill for up to 2 hours before slicing and serving on plates.

80 Ricotta Hotcakes with Bananas and Honeycomb Butter

BILL GRANGER
DESSERTS

Serves 6–8

275 g/10 oz ricotta cheese

175 ml/6 fl oz milk

4 eggs, separated

150 g/5 oz plain flour

pinch of salt

1 tsp baking powder

50 g/2 oz unsalted butter

6–8 bananas

icing sugar, to dust

FOR THE HONEYCOMB BUTTER:

250 g/9 oz unsalted butter, softened

100 g/4 oz honeycomb

2 tbsp clear honey

Born in America, the hotcake has assimilated well into breakfast society in Australia, which is where I'm from. Here I've dressed up hotcakes by substituting maple syrup with a gold-flecked, crunch-sensation butter. Any leftovers would be great on toast. The batter can be stored happily for up to 24 hours covered with cling film in the fridge.

1 To make the honeycomb butter, place the butter, honeycomb and honey in a food processor or liquidizer and blend until smooth. Using a plastic spatula, transfer on to a sheet of non-stick baking parchment, shape into a roll about 4 cm/1½ in thick, and wrap up tightly. Chill for at least 2 hours – overnight is best – until firm.

2 Place the ricotta in a large bowl and mix in the milk and egg yolks. Sift the flour, salt and baking powder into a separate bowl and then fold into the ricotta mixture until just combined. Place the egg whites in a clean, dry bowl and beat until stiff peaks form. Using a large metal spoon, fold half into the ricotta mixture to loosen the mix and then fold in the remaining half until just combined.

3 Heat a large non-stick frying pan. Lightly grease with a small portion of the butter and drop two tablespoons per hotcake into the pan – don't try to cook more than three in one batch. Cook over a low to medium heat for 2 minutes or until golden, then turn over and cook for another minute or so until puffed up and golden. Loosely wrap in a clean tea towel while you finish cooking the remainder.

4 Slice each banana lengthways on to a plate and stack three hotcakes on top with a couple of slices of honeycomb butter. Dust with icing sugar and serve immediately.

81 Chocolate Brownie Berry Trifle

SUE LAWRENCE
DESSERTS

Serves 6–8

350 g/12 oz plain chocolate
(at least 55–60% cocoa solids)

200 g/7 oz unsalted butter,
plus extra for greasing

3 large eggs

250 g/9 oz dark muscovado
sugar

100g/4 oz plain flour, sifted

1 tsp baking powder

pinch of salt

175 g/6 oz raspberries

FOR THE TRIFLE:

500 g/1lb 2 oz raspberries

4–5 tbsp Drambuie

3 large eggs

500 g/1 lb 2 oz mascarpone

100 g/4 oz golden caster sugar

100 g/4 oz blueberries

50 g/2 oz plain chocolate,
coarsely grated (55–60%
cocoa solids)

This dessert is decadently rich, so small portions should be offered… at least to start with. Use plain chocolate with about 55 to 60 per cent cocoa solids; one with 70 per cent would be too bitter for the sweet, gooey, almost fudge-like brownies. It is seriously tempting to remove the brownies from the tin when they are still warm but they are far too fragile to decant until cold. The trifle will last well in the fridge for several days, although the texture becomes more solid.

1 Preheat the oven to 170°C/325°F/Gas Mark 3 (fan oven 150°C from cold). To make the brownies, butter a 23 cm/9 in square cake tin. Melt the chocolate and butter together in a heatproof bowl set over a pan of simmering water; then set aside to cool slightly.

2 Using an electric beater or balloon whisk, whisk the eggs in a large bowl until thickened, then gradually add the muscovado sugar and beat until glossy. Beat in the cooled melted chocolate mixture, then gently fold in the sifted flour, baking powder and salt.

3 Pour just over half the brownie mixture into the prepared cake tin. Scatter over the raspberries, then cover with the remaining mixture. Bake for about 40 minutes or until the surface is set and slightly cracked. To test, pierce the middle with a fine skewer – it should come out with just a little mixture sticking to it. Place the cake tin on a wire rack and allow it to rest for about 20 minutes, then cut the brownie into squares and remove them from the tin when cold.

4 To make the trifle, break each brownie in half and place in the base of a glass trifle bowl. Top with the raspberries and slowly drizzle over the Drambuie.

5 Separate the eggs and place the yolks in a bowl with the mascarpone and sugar, then beat until smooth. Whisk the egg whites in a separate bowl until stiff and then gently fold into the mascarpone mixture, starting with a small amount to lighten the mixture. Spread the mascarpone mixture over the brownies and raspberries; cover with cling film. Chill for at least 8 hours to set (overnight is best). To serve, decorate with the blueberries and scatter over the grated chocolate.

82 Rhubarb and Orange Syllabub with Toasted Nuts

MERRILEES PARKER
DESSERTS

Serves 4

3 tbsp Grand Marnier (orange-flavoured liqueur)

3 tbsp Seville orange marmalade (good quality)

grated rind of 1 orange (ideally Seville)

150 ml/¼ pint double cream

300 ml/½ pint mascarpone

100 g/4 oz pistachio nuts

4 tbsp orange blossom honey

FOR THE RHUBARB:

225 g/8 oz fresh rhubarb stalks

75 g/3 oz sugar

1 vanilla pod

This is a great dessert for when you have people round for dinner because you can make it in advance and just top with the toasted nuts when ready to serve. Roasting rhubarb in the oven rather than stewing it is a great way to keep its shape. Home-grown rhubarb that arrives early in the year is known as 'forced' rhubarb; this is achieved either by covering the plant with a pot to encourage early growth in the spring or, more commonly, by growing it in a hothouse. Look out for Champagne rhubarb, which is the sweetest variety of all. It comes very early in spring and has slim, tender stalks.

1 Preheat the oven to 200°C/400°F/Gas Mark 6 (fan oven 180°C from cold). To cook the rhubarb, trim the ends from each piece of fruit and cut in half if it is very long. Place in a roasting tin and sprinkle over the sugar. Run a knife through the centre of the vanilla pod and place it on top. Cover the tin with foil and seal well. Roast for 20 minutes, then remove from the oven but leave the foil in place for 10 minutes. Leave to cool.

2 Mix the Grand Marnier in a small bowl with the marmalade and orange rind. Place the cream in a large bowl and mix in the mascarpone, then gently stir in the marmalade mixture and finally gently fold in the cooked rhubarb. Divide the mixture among wine glasses and chill for at least 4 hours, but preferably overnight.

3 Place the pistachio nuts in a dry frying pan and cook for a few minutes, tossing occasionally until toasted. Tip on to a plate and leave to cool completely, then roughly chop. To serve, sprinkle the pistachio nuts over each syllabub and drizzle the orange blossom honey on top.

83 Cranberry and Raspberry Jellies

LESLEY WATERS
DESSERTS

Serves 4

9 tbsp cranberry and raspberry cordial, plus extra for drizzling

11 g sachet powdered gelatine

150 g/5 oz raspberries

100 g/4 oz blueberries

These lovely translucent jellies look stunning with the berries twinkling through, and they are really refreshing too. Pour a little extra cordial over just before serving. The idea is that as you take your first bite you get this fantastic hit of cranberry in your mouth.

1 Dilute the cranberry and raspberry cordial in a jug with 600 ml/1 pint of cold water. Measure four tablespoons into a small pan and sprinkle over the gelatine. Set aside for 10 minutes to allow the gelatine to 'sponge'.

2 Place the pan over a gentle heat and swirl the pan until the gelatine has completely dissolved. Do not allow the gelatine to boil, as that will prevent it from setting. Pour in the remaining diluted cordial and stir well over a gentle heat.

3 Arrange the raspberries and blueberries in four tumblers or wine glasses. Carefully pour over the dissolved gelatine mixture, trying not to disturb the fruit too much. Leave to cool completely and then chill for 3 hours until softly set. Drizzle over a little extra cordial and set each glass on a plate to serve.

84 Espresso Crème Brûlée

Serves 4

3 tsp instant coffee (good quality)

500 ml/18 fl oz milk

450 ml/¾ pint double cream

½ vanilla pod, split in half

1 egg

4 egg yolks

50 g/2 oz caster sugar

75 g/3 oz mascarpone cheese

about 75 g/3 oz Demerara sugar

This recipe is a variation on one of my favourite desserts, which is normally only flavoured with vanilla. However, this version works very well and offers a fantastic finish to a dinner party. Try to use instant espresso coffee granules as they have that fantastic bitter edge.

1 Place the coffee, milk, cream and vanilla pod in a pan and slowly bring to the boil. Place the egg, yolks, caster sugar and mascarpone in a bowl and whisk with an electric mixer until the mixture is very pale and thick.

2 Just before the coffee mixture boils over the sides of the pan, pour it on to the egg and sugar mixture, whisking continuously until well combined. Strain back into the pan through a muslin-lined sieve and stir over a low heat for 2–3 minutes until it is thick and coats the back of a spoon.

3 Remove the pan from the heat and continue to stir for another couple of minutes. Pour into martini glasses or ramekins, taking the mixture right up to the top. Leave them to set in the fridge for at least 3–4 hours, or preferably overnight.

4 To serve, preheat the grill to its highest setting (or you can use a blowtorch). Sprinkle the tops of the brûlées with the Demerara sugar, making sure you take it right to the edges of the containers, and slide them under the grill for 2–3 minutes until the sugar has caramelized. Remove and leave until the sugar topping has cooled and gone hard before serving.

85 Hot and Cold Ice Cream with Griddled Figs and Bananas

JAMES MARTIN
DESSERTS

Serves 4

1 egg

pinch of salt

8 filo pastry sheets, thawed if frozen

4 scoops vanilla ice cream, frozen solid

icing sugar, for dusting

25 g/1 oz unsalted butter

4 figs

2 bananas

4 tbsp clear honey

fresh mint sprigs, to decorate

Here is a way of dressing up the humble banana and some fresh figs. It is served with the unusual but heavenly addition of baked ice cream. I can promise you that when this is served, no-one will ever guess that you haven't been slaving away for hours in the kitchen.

1 Preheat the oven to 190°C/375°F/Gas Mark 5 (fan oven 170°C from cold). Heat a heavy-based griddle pan. Break the egg into a bowl and add the salt. Beat with a fork, then pass through a tea strainer into a small bowl. Unroll the filo and cut into 12 x 10 cm/4 in squares. Layer up three squares of the filo at slight angles to each other and brush the edges with some of the egg wash.

2 Place a scoop of ice cream in the centre of one of the layered-up filo squares and draw the pastry edges around the filling, pinching the tops together to form a little 'purse'. Keep in the freezer while you make the remaining purses.

3 Arrange the filo purses on a non-stick baking sheet and egg-wash them all over, then dust with icing sugar and bake for about 3 minutes or until the pastry is cooked and lightly browned but the ice cream is still solid in the middle.

4 Meanwhile, melt the butter in a small pan or in the microwave. Cut the figs in half and peel the bananas and cut them in half as well. Brush with the melted butter and add to the heated griddle pan. Cook for a minute or two on each side and then arrange on plates. Drizzle a little of the honey on each serving. Add a filo purse to the side of each and dust with icing sugar. Decorate with mint sprigs to serve.

86 Butternut Squash Fruitcake and Whipped Cream

ANTONY WORRALL
THOMPSON
BAKING

Serves 10–12

50 g/2 oz sultanas

50 ml/2 fl oz dark rum

1 kg/2¼ lb butternut squash, halved and seeded

250 g/9 oz unsalted butter, softened, plus extra for greasing

caster sugar, for dusting

600 g/1 lb 5 oz light muscovado sugar

juice of 2 oranges

50 g/2 oz ready-to-eat dried cherries

50 g/2 oz ready-to-eat dried cranberries

50 g/2 oz ready-to-eat dried dates, stoned and chopped

100 g/4 oz walnuts, chopped

grated rind of 1 orange and 1 lemon (preferably unwaxed)

continued opposite

This recipe has a Jamaican influence and makes a good alternative to Christmas cake. The butternut squash is roasted both to caramelize its natural sweetness and to soften it before puréeing. Buttermilk is available in most major supermarkets but milk mixed with the juice of a lemon and left to curdle for 20 minutes is a good alternative.

1 Place the sultanas in a small bowl and pour over the rum to cover. Cover with cling film and set aside at room temperature overnight to allow the sultanas to plump up. The next day drain the sultanas, reserving the rum, and set aside in separate bowls.

2 Preheat the oven to 190°C/375°F/Gas Mark 5 (fan oven 170°C from cold). Cut the narrow top end off the butternut squash and peel away the skin. Grate the flesh – you'll need 75 g/3 oz in total.

3 Cut the rest of the butternut squash in half and scoop out the seeds. Smear the flesh with 25 g/1 oz of the butter and arrange on a baking sheet. Roast for about 1 hour or until completely tender when pierced with a fine skewer. Remove from the oven and leave to cool, then scoop out the flesh into a food processor or liquidizer, discarding the skin. Blend to a purée – you'll need 225 g/8 oz in total.

4 Reduce the oven temperature to 180°C/350°F/Gas Mark 4 (fan oven 160°C). Butter a 23 cm/9 in loose-bottomed cake tin and dust lightly with caster sugar. Place the reserved rum in a small pan and stir in 200 g/7 oz of the muscovado sugar and the orange juice, stirring over a gentle heat until the sugar has dissolved. Set aside.

5 Add the reserved grated butternut squash to the soaked sultanas with the cherries, cranberries, dates, walnuts, orange and lemon rind. Add one tablespoon of the flour, mix to combine and set aside.

6 Beat the remaining 225 g/8 oz of butter in a bowl with an electric beater until light and fluffy. Slowly beat in the remaining 400 g/14 oz of muscovado sugar. Add the eggs one at a time, beating thoroughly after each addition. Fold in the butternut squash purée.

118

4 large eggs

400 g/14 oz plain flour

1 tsp baking powder

½ tsp salt

1½ tsp ground cinnamon

good pinch of freshly grated nutmeg

1 tsp ground ginger

1 tsp bicarbonate of soda

300 ml/½ pint buttermilk

icing sugar, to dust (optional)

whipped cream, to serve

7 Sift the remaining flour into a bowl with the baking powder, salt, cinnamon, nutmeg and ginger. Combine the bicarbonate of soda with the buttermilk in a jug. Stir one third of the flour mixture and a third of the buttermilk into the butternut squash purée mixture and repeat in the same quantities until the ingredients are used up. Finally fold in the dried fruit and nut mixture and spoon into the prepared cake tin. Bake for 1½–2 hours until cooked through and golden brown, or until a fine skewer comes out clean when inserted into the middle of the cake – you may need to cover the cake with foil halfway through to prevent the top from burning.

8 Remove the cake from the oven and leave it to rest for 10–15 minutes, then prick it all over with a fine skewer. Drizzle over the reserved rum mixture while the cake is still warm. Transfer to a serving plate and dust with icing sugar, if liked. Cut into slices and add a dollop of whipped cream to serve.

87 Macaroon Cake with Lemon Curd Yoghurt Cream

SUE LAWRENCE
BAKING

Serves 8

150 g/5 oz butter, slightly softened, plus extra for greasing

150 g/5 oz ground almonds

100 g/4 oz plain flour, sifted

100 g/4 oz golden caster sugar

grated rind of 1 lemon (preferably unwaxed)

FOR THE FILLING:

40 g/1½ oz unsalted butter

5 large eggs

300 g/11 oz desiccated
coconut

300 g/11 oz golden caster sugar

grated rind and juice of 1 large
lemon

**FOR THE LEMON CURD
YOGHURT CREAM:**

200 g/7 oz plain yoghurt
(runny, not the set variety)

1–2 tbsp lemon curd (preferably
home-made)

This is a gorgeous, moist coconut cake with a lemony almond base
and light crunchy crust. It is perfect for afternoon tea but also delicious served for pudding with seasonal berries and a dollop of the
lemon curd yoghurt cream. Home-made lemon curd is nothing like
the garish yellow shop-bought variety, and it does not take long to
make. Simply mix three eggs with the juice and rind of three large
lemons in a large heatproof bowl. Mix in 100 g/4 oz of butter and 225 g/
8 oz of caster sugar and set over a pan of simmering water. Cook
gently for about 20 minutes, stirring constantly until thickened, then
cool and use as required. It will last for up to 6 weeks in the fridge.

1 Preheat the oven to 170°C/325°F/Gas Mark 3 (fan oven 150°C from cold).
Butter a 24 cm/9½ in loose-bottomed cake tin. To make the base, place the
almonds, flour and golden caster sugar in a food processor and blend to combine.

2 Add the butter to the food processor with the lemon rind and process briefly
until the mixture looks as if you could bring it together in your hands. Tip into the
prepared cake tin and press it well into the base and a little way up the sides.

3 To make the filling, melt the butter in a small pan or in the microwave. Leave to
cool. Separate the eggs and place the yolks in a bowl. Add the melted butter and
coconut to the yolks and beat together until well blended. Whisk the egg whites
in a separate bowl until stiff, and then gradually beat in the sugar, a spoonful at a
time, until glossy. Fold in the lemon rind and juice until just combined. Gently fold
the meringue into the coconut mixture.

4 Spoon the filling into the prepared base and bake for about 1 hour or until the
cake is lightly golden and just firm to the touch. Place the cake tin on a wire rack
to cool completely, then transfer the cake to a serving plate.

5 To make the lemon curd yoghurt cream, place the yoghurt in a bowl and beat
in enough of the lemon curd to taste. Cut the macaroon cake into slices and
arrange on plates. Serve with a dollop of the lemon curd yoghurt cream on the side.

88 Welsh Cakes

LIZ SCOURFIELD
BAKING

Makes about 12

225 g/8 oz self-raising flour, plus a little extra for dusting

100 g/4 oz butter, diced, plus a little extra for griddling (Welsh salted, if possible)

75 g/3 oz caster sugar, plus extra for dusting

50 g/2 oz sultanas

1 egg

a little milk, if necessary

This recipe is from my auntie Moira – she taught me how to make these traditional delicacies. Once the liquid is added the ingredients should be mixed with the blade of a kitchen knife. The cutting action mixes the ingredients and prevents the air incorporated during the rubbing-in process from being knocked out. The dough should be handled lightly to prevent toughening. Overhandling results in hard, leathery cakes. When cooked, the Welsh cakes should be golden brown (although some people I know like them almost burnt). The texture should be soft and light, more like bread than cake.

1 Sift the flour into a large bowl and rub in the butter until the mixture resembles fine breadcrumbs. Stir in the caster sugar and sultanas. Make a well in the centre and break in the egg. Mix with a round-bladed knife to a soft dough, adding a splash of milk if necessary.

2 Roll out the dough on a lightly floured work surface to a 0.5 cm/¼ in thickness and stamp out rounds using a 7.5–10 cm/3–4 in fluted cutter. Rub a cast-iron flat griddle pan or large frying pan with butter and wipe away excess. Place on a low heat and leave to become moderately hot.

3 Add the Welsh cakes to the heated griddle and cook for 2–3 minutes on each side until puffed up and golden brown, turning once with a palette knife – you may have to do this in batches, depending on the size of your pan. Dust with caster sugar while they are still warm and pile high on a plate to serve.

89 Chocolate Chip Muffins

PAUL HOLLYWOOD
BAKING

Makes about 6

100 g/4 oz unsalted butter (plus extra for greasing – optional)

75 g/3 oz caster sugar

2 eggs, lightly beaten

100 g/4 oz strong white flour

2 tsp baking powder

100 g/4 oz chocolate chips

25 g/1 oz cocoa powder

about 50 ml/2 fl oz milk

chilled whipped cream, to serve

These muffins are incredibly easy to make in a freestanding electric mixer, but obviously you could use a hand-held electric beater or even a wooden spoon – you'll just need a lot more elbow grease. If you've got a non-stick tin, don't bother with the paper cases; just give all the holes a light greasing with a little butter.

1 Preheat the oven to 200°C/400°F/Gas Mark 6 (fan oven 180°C from cold). Line a 6-hole deep bun or muffin tin with paper cases, or use a non-stick tin and lightly grease. Place the butter in the bowl of a freestanding electric mixer with the sugar and cream them together until light and fluffy. Gradually add the eggs and continue to mix for 3 minutes until well combined.

2 Tip the flour into the mixer with the baking powder, chocolate chips, cocoa powder and a splash of milk. Continue to mix for another 3 minutes until well combined. Spoon the mixture into the paper cases (or direct into a non-stick tin), piling it up in the centre, and bake for about 15 minutes or until the muffins are well risen and craggy in appearance. Transfer to a wire rack to cool a little and serve warm or cold on plates with a dollop of the whipped cream.

90 Real Fruit Tea Cakes

PAUL HOLLYWOOD
BAKING

Makes about 14

500 g/1 lb 2 oz strong white unbleached flour, plus extra for dusting

25 g/1 oz fresh yeast or 2 x 7g sachets easy-blend dried yeast, about 1 tbsp in total

2 tsp salt

1 tbsp ground cinnamon

75 g/3 oz caster sugar

50 g/2 oz butter, melted

about 300 ml/¹⁄₂ pint lukewarm water

50 g/2 oz sultanas

50 g/2 oz glacé cherries

2 mandarins, separated into segments and chopped

1 eating apple, peeled, cored and chopped (tossed in a little lemon juice to prevent discoloration)

1 egg, beaten

pot of butter, to serve

This classic English favourite – light and airy buns studded with dried and fresh fruit – is really a cross between bread and cake. Allow plenty of time for them to rise and prove – the length of time it takes depends on where the dough is left. I just love to eat them with lashings of butter for afternoon tea.

1 Sift the flour into a large bowl with the yeast, salt, cinnamon and sugar. Stir the melted butter into the dry ingredients, then pour in enough of the water to make a soft dough. Turn out on to a floured surface and lightly flour your hands. Knead for about 5 minutes until the dough is smooth and pliable. Place in a lightly buttered bowl, which should be large enough to allow the dough to double in bulk. Cover with cling film and set aside in a warm place for about 1¹⁄₂ hours or until doubled in size.

2 When the dough has doubled in size, remove the cling film and knock back with a clenched fist. Tip on to a lightly floured board and sprinkle over the sultanas, cherries, mandarins and apple and knead thoroughly until evenly combined. Using lightly floured hands, pull off 90 g/3¹⁄₂ oz pieces of dough and roll each one between your palms to make a neat bun. Arrange on large baking sheets that are lined with non-stick parchment paper – you should have about 14 in total – making sure they are well spaced apart. Flatten the top of each one gently with a rolling pin and then brush with the beaten egg. Cover with damp tea towels and leave to rise at warm room temperature until doubled in size, about 1 hour.

3 Meanwhile, preheat the oven to 200°C/400°F/Gas Mark 6 (fan oven 180°C from cold). Bake for 15 minutes until well risen and golden brown, covering with foil if necessary to prevent over-browning. The cooked tea cakes should sound hollow when tapped underneath. Transfer to a wire rack to cool and then pile on to a plate to serve. Hand around a small pot of butter for spreading separately.

91 Amaretti Biscuits

GINO D'ACAMPO
BAKING

Makes about 40 biscuits

4 egg whites

350 g/12 oz caster sugar

350 g/12 oz ground almonds

2 tbsp Amaretto liqueur

25 g/1 oz unsalted butter

shots of Italian coffee or ice cream, to serve

These biscuits are usually eaten as an after-dinner treat with a good shot of strong Italian coffee. They are good with ice cream too – coffee ice cream in particular. For an instant dessert, try crumbling them into a glass dish, placing a scoop of coffee ice cream on top, then adding another layer of crumbled amaretti and another scoop of the ice cream. Top with a swirl of whipped cream and decorate with a whole amaretti biscuit. For a special occasion, dip half of each biscuit in melted plain chocolate and leave to harden.

1 Place the egg whites in a large bowl and beat with an electric mixer until stiff and firm. Gradually add the caster sugar, a tablespoon at a time, and then fold in the ground almonds until you have achieved a thick, glossy mixture. Stir in the Amaretto liqueur.

2 Melt the butter in a small pan or in the microwave. Line large baking sheets with non-stick baking paper and then brush over the melted butter. Using a tea-spoon, place small heaps of the almond mixture about 2 cm/$^3/_4$ in apart to allow them to expand while cooking.

3 Bake the biscuits for 10–15 minutes until golden brown. Eat warm or leave to cool on a wire rack until firm and crispy. Serve them with a good strong shot of Italian coffee or some of your favourite ice cream.

92 Shortbread

SUE LAWRENCE
BAKING

Makes 20–24 pieces

225 g/8 oz butter, softened, plus extra for greasing

100 g/4 oz golden caster sugar

225 g/8 oz plain flour, sifted, plus extra for dusting

125 g/4½ oz cornflour, sifted

caster sugar, to dredge

This shortbread will keep well in an airtight tin for up to one week and is just the thing with a cup of morning coffee. After lots of experimenting I found that a slightly salted butter gives the best flavour. When I was working as an assistant in a *lycée* in the French Pyrenees I often made shortbread for the pupils and staff. They loved it but always said how rich it was, while to me it was simple and delicious yet such a part of my life as to be almost mundane. But considering that it was originally a special-occasion biscuit (unlike the plainer bannocks and oatcakes) that has gradually become mainstream, it's perhaps not surprising that first-timers consider it rich.

1 Preheat the oven to 150°C/300°F/Gas Mark 2 (fan oven 130°C from cold). Butter a 23 x 33 cm/9 x 13 in Swiss roll tin. Place the butter and golden caster sugar in a food processor or a freestanding electric mixer and blend until pale and fluffy.

2 Add the sifted flour and cornflour and blend the mixture briefly again, just until thoroughly combined. Tip the mixture into the prepared Swiss roll tin and, using floured hands, press down so it is level all over.

3 Prick all over with a fork (do this carefully, so that you do not disturb the level surface) and then bake for 50–60 minutes. What you are looking for is a uniform pale golden all over. Do not allow it to become golden brown.

4 Remove the shortbread from the oven and dredge all over with caster sugar then cut into squares. Leave for 5 minutes or so then carefully transfer to a wire rack to cool completely. Store in an airtight tin until ready to serve.

93 Spiced Oat Biscuits

ANTONY WORRALL
THOMPSON
BAKING

Makes about 12

75 g/3 oz vegetable margarine, plus extra for greasing

75 g/3 oz wholemeal flour, plus a little extra for dusting

½ tsp salt

50 g/2 oz porridge oats

½ tsp bicarbonate of soda

½ tsp ground mixed spice

50 g/2 oz pear and apple spread (from a jar)

When my children got the baking bug I set them up to make these simple biscuits. The great part about them is that they don't use any refined sugar. Instead, I've used pear and apple spread, which is available in jars from health food shops and most supermarkets. The hard part (for the kids) was waiting until they were cooled and crisp before eating them. In the unlikely event that there are any left over, they should be stored in an airtight jar or they will go soft again.

1 Preheat the oven to 190°C/375°F/Gas Mark 5 (fan oven 170°C from cold). Grease two baking sheets and lightly dust them with flour. Sift the flour and salt into a bowl, tipping in any wholemeal flakes that get left in the sieve. Stir in the oats, bicarbonate of soda and mixed spice.

2 Cream the margarine in a separate large bowl and beat in the pear and apple spread, a little at a time until well combined. Beat in the oat mixture until well combined.

3 Place walnut-sized portions of the biscuit mixture on to the prepared baking sheets, leaving a 5 cm/2 in space around each one, and then flatten each one slightly with a fork. Bake for 15 minutes or until they are beginning to turn golden brown. Remove from the oven and leave to cool completely on the baking sheets. Arrange on a plate to serve, or store in an airtight container.

94 Mum's Soda Bread

TONY TOBIN
BAKING

Makes 1 loaf

450 g/1 lb wholemeal flour

225 g/8 oz self-raising flour, plus extra for dusting

1½ tsp bicarbonate of soda

1½ tsp cream of tartar

pinch of salt

2 tsp sugar

600 ml/1 pint milk

250 ml/9 fl oz plain yoghurt

This recipe is straight from my mum and is the one she used to bake for us all the time when we were growing up. I just love it straight out of the oven, or fried in the morning with an egg. Otherwise, cool on a wire rack or, if you like a soft crust, wrap in a linen or cotton tea towel.

1 Preheat the oven to 190°C/375°F/Gas Mark 5 (fan oven 170°C from cold). Mix the wholemeal flour in a bowl with the self-raising flour, bicarbonate of soda, cream of tartar, salt and sugar.

2 Mix together the milk and yoghurt in a jug and mix enough into the flour mixture to make a soft dough. Flour your hands and the work surface, and knead lightly until the dough is smooth.

3 Shape the dough into a circle about 4 cm/1½ in deep. Take a sharp, well-floured knife and cut a deep cross in the top. Place on a baking sheet and bake for 45 minutes until crusty and golden brown. To test whether it's ready, tap the bottom and listen for a hollow sound.

95 Focaccia Stuffed with Tomato, Ricotta and Pesto

MIKE ROBINSON
BAKING

Serves 10–12

4 red peppers

about 150 ml/¼ pint olive oil, plus extra for brushing

75 g/3 oz pine nuts

continued overleaf

People just can't seem to get enough of flavoured breads and this one is a real winner. I devised this recipe when I used to run a deli and it was always the first thing to sell out, especially on Sunday mornings.

1 Preheat the grill. Arrange the red peppers on a grill rack and cook for 20–30 minutes until well charred and blistered, turning regularly. Transfer to a polythene bag and secure with a knot. Leave the peppers to cool completely, then peel. Slice the flesh, discarding the seeds and cores. Place in a bowl and add about 50 ml/2 fl oz of olive oil to cover. Set aside until needed.

Baking

large bunch of fresh basil,
leaves stripped

2 garlic cloves, peeled

225 g/8 oz freshly grated
Parmesan

750 g/1¾ lb strong white
unbleached flour, plus extra for
dusting

2 x 7g sachets easy-blend dried
yeast, about 1 tbsp in total

1 tbsp caster sugar

about 600 ml/1 pint hand-hot
water

250 g/9 oz ricotta cheese

150 g/5 oz cherry tomatoes,
halved

25 g/1 oz rocket leaves

1 tbsp roughly chopped fresh
rosemary

Maldon sea salt and freshly
ground black pepper

2 Heat a small heavy-based frying pan. Add the pine nuts and toast until golden
brown, tossing occasionally. Tip out on to a plate and leave to cool completely. To
make the pesto, place 25 g/1 oz of the pine nuts in a food processor or liquidizer
with the basil, garlic and half of the Parmesan. Blend briefly and then pour in
enough of the olive oil through the feeder tube to make a smooth purée – you'll
probably need about 75 ml/3 fl oz in total. Transfer to a bowl and season to taste.
Cover with cling film and chill until needed.

3 Place the flour in the bowl of a food mixer fitted with a dough attachment. Add
the yeast with the sugar, lukewarm water and a teaspoon of salt. Switch on the
machine and mix until you have a very sloppy dough. Turn out on to a well-floured
surface; lightly flour your hands. Knead for about 10 minutes until the dough is
smooth and pliable. Lightly oil a bowl, which should be large enough for the
dough to triple in bulk. Place the dough in the bowl and lightly oil the top. Cover
with cling film and set aside in a warm place for 1–2 hours until it has tripled in size.

4 Preheat the oven to 220°C/425°F/Gas Mark 7 (fan oven 200°C from cold).
When the dough has tripled in size, remove the cling film and, with a fist, punch
it down. Remove from the bowl and place it on an oiled work surface. Knead
for a couple of minutes until smooth, then roll out to a large rectangle, about
0.5 cm/¼ in thick. Spread over the pesto and then add a thick layer of the
ricotta. Scatter the remaining pine nuts and Parmesan on top with the roasted
peppers, cherry tomatoes and rocket leaves.

5 Roll the dough up like a Swiss roll, tucking the ends in, and place on a well-
oiled baking sheet with the join underneath. Dimple the surface and brush with
oil. Scatter the rosemary on top with a good sprinkling of salt. Bake for about
40 minutes or until cooked through and pale golden. Check its progress during
cooking and if it looks like it's starting to burn, turn the oven down. Transfer to a
wire rack and leave to cool a little, then cut into wedges and pile into a bread
basket to serve.

96 Mango Lassi

MANJU MALHI
DRINKS

Serves 2

**1 ripe mango or 400 g/14 oz
can mango slices in syrup,
drained**

125 ml/4 fl oz milk

175 ml/6 fl oz natural yoghurt

2 tsp sugar

ice cubes, to serve

This has to be the most popular Indian drink. It can be either sweet
or salted, and occasionally it's spiced. I prefer mine simple and sweet
and often blend it with some fresh fruit, such as the mango I've used
below. Alternatively, try adding a handful of strawberries and a sliced
banana, or, for a creamier, thicker drink, add two tablespoons of
cream before whizzing in the blender. I always find once you've
started drinking it, you just can't stop...

1 If you have a fresh mango, use a vegetable peeler to remove the skin, then cut
away all the flesh from the stone. Place the mango in a food processor or liquidizer
with the milk, yoghurt and sugar. Blend until smooth, then pour into tall glasses
and add a couple of ice cubes to each one to serve.

97 Soup Smoothie

LESLEY WATERS
DRINKS

Serves 2

1 large ripe mango

50 ml/2 fl oz freshly squeezed orange juice

grated rind and juice of ½ lime

1 banana

2 tbsp plain yoghurt

1 ready-made meringue nest

50 g/2 oz small strawberries, halved

1 ripe passion fruit

This is my idea of a treat any day of the week – and it's a great way to get children to eat plenty of fruit. I've adapted it from my family's favourite smoothie, which we like to eat from bowls with a spoon as it's so thick with all its fruit. This is a fantastic finale to any meal, whether you are trying to be healthy or not, and the real beauty of it is that it's made in minutes.

1 Peel the mango and cut away the flesh from the stone. Dice a little – a heaped tablespoon's worth – and set aside. Place the remainder in a food processor or liquidizer with the orange juice and lime rind and juice. Peel the banana and slice straight into the food processor and blend until smooth.

2 Pour the smoothie into soup bowls and drizzle over the yoghurt. Crumble the meringue on top and scatter over the reserved mango and the strawberries. Cut the passion fruit in half and squeeze the seeds on top. Serve at once.

98 Bloody Mary Shots

MERRILEES PARKER
DRINKS

Makes about 20

150 ml/¼ pint vodka, well chilled

250 ml/9 fl oz thin tomato juice, chilled (from a can is best)

juice of 1 lime

2 tsp freshly grated horseradish

1 tsp celery salt

a good shake of Tabasco

1 tbsp Worcestershire sauce

1 mini cucumber, peeled, sliced and cut into very fine juliennes

1 tsp cracked back pepper

This makes about 450 ml/¾ pint, and if you want to use it immediately, mix it in a cocktail shaker with a handful of ice cubes. I often prepare the seasoned tomato juice and stick it in the fridge – it keeps for a couple of weeks and then I've always got some to hand! Surprisingly, the best results are achieved with (cheaper) tomato juice from a can because it's much thinner than the more expensive juices that come in cartons. However, the real secret is in the seasonings, which you'll need to experiment with until you find the perfect balance to suit you.

1 Place shot glasses in the freezer to chill. Place the vodka in a jug with the tomato and lime juice. Season with the horseradish, celery salt, Tabasco and Worcestershire sauce, stirring well to combine. Cover the top of the jug with cling film and chill until ready to serve.

2 To serve, place the glasses on a plate or tray. Give the bloody Mary mix a good stir and check the seasoning, then pour into the glasses. Finish each one with a little cucumber julienne and a pinch of the black pepper.

99 Sogni Di Notte (Dreams of the Night)

Serves 2

3 tbsp vodka

3 tbsp Tia Maria (coffee liqueur)

1 tbsp Amaretto liqueur

6 tbsp single cream

about 50 g/2 oz crushed ice

This cocktail arouses strong memories of my childhood. My father would order it and I would beg him for a small sip. Sometimes he would give in to my pleas; no wonder it's now my favourite cocktail.

1 Place the vodka in a cocktail shaker with the Tia Maria, Amaretto and cream. Add a good handful of crushed ice and shake until thoroughly combined. Strain into Martini glasses and serve at once.

100 Ruby Grapefruit and Juniper Granita

JEANNE RANKIN
DRINKS

Serves 4–6

325 ml/11 fl oz still mineral water

200 g/7 oz caster sugar

6 juniper berries, lightly crushed

2 ruby grapefruits

250 ml/9 fl oz freshly squeezed ruby grapefruit juice

1–2 tbsp gin

Drinks

This is really a cross between a drink and a dessert, but it can also be served as a between-course palette cleanser with its sharp, cool and refreshing taste. For me, it's a great alternative to sweet puddings, and looks like sparkling jewels when you serve it piled up in martini glasses. But the best bit is it is low in calories!

1 Place four martini glasses in the freezer to chill thoroughly. Pour 125 ml/4$\frac{1}{2}$ fl oz of the water in a pan with 50 g/2 oz of the sugar and the juniper berries. Bring to the boil, stirring until the sugar has dissolved, then remove from the heat and leave to infuse for 30 minutes.

2 Place the remaining 200 ml/7 fl oz of water in a separate small pan with the remaining 150 g/5 oz of sugar. Bring to the boil, stirring until the sugar has dissolved, then remove from the heat and leave to cool a little.

3 Holding one of the grapefruit over a bowl to catch any juices, peel and segment it using a sharp serrated knife, discarding all pith. Put the flesh in the bowl and repeat with the remaining grapefruit. Pour over the sugar syrup, stirring to combine, then cover with cling film and chill in the fridge for at least 30 minutes (or overnight is fine) to allow the flavours to infuse.

4 Strain the juniper-berry-infused sugar syrup through a fine sieve into the grapefruit juice, then add the gin to taste. Pour this into a wide and shallow polythene container, cover with a lid and place in the freezer for about 1 hour, or until the granita starts to freeze and form crystals. Take a large fork and scrape the sides and mix gently to combine the more frozen parts with the less frozen. Continue to stir occasionally during freezing in order to create a true granita texture: a complete snow of tiny ice crystals. It will take about three hours for it all to set sufficiently.

5 To serve, place a few segments of the marinated grapefruit in each chilled martini glass. Using an ice cream scoop, add a spoonful or two of the granita and top with a few more of the marinated grapefruit segments. Drizzle a tablespoon of the sugar syrup used to marinate the grapefruit over the fruit and granita and serve at once.

Who's Who on *Saturday Kitchen*

Rosa is a woman of our times. In her early thirties and living in north London, she is married to musician/composer/record producer Ed and has three sons. For the past nine years she has been juggling motherhood with a career as a criminal barrister and only entered the *Masterchef 2001* competition as a dare. The youngest of four, she spent hours in the Sussex family home's kitchen where her mother taught her to bake when she was just eight. Young Rosa took over more and more of the family cooking, teaching herself the basic skills as she went along, inspired by her father, her grandmother and Great-aunt Agnes. Rosa's cooking now is still very much for family and friends. She likes simple, clean flavours and (fairly!) elegant presentation.

ED BAINES

Ed Baines is chef and co-owner of Randall and Aubin, the champagne and oyster bar in London's Soho. His career started with a two-year apprenticeship at the Dorchester, followed by three years of cooking on yachts and in hotels from Juan-les-Pins to Queensland. He then headed back to London to work at Bibendum and the River Café. At 25, he became head chef at Daphne's in South Kensington, where he stayed for three years. He opened Randall and Aubin with his friend James Poulton in 1996, and followed it with Ifield in Chelsea, another Randall and Aubin in Fulham Road, and The Belsize. Ed has appeared on *Good Food Live*, *Cupid's Dinners*,

Housecall, *Countdown to Christmas*, *Granada Livetime*, Central Television and the Carlton Food network. He has presented his own series, *Lunch with Ed Baines* and *Ed Baines Entertains*, and his first book, *Entertain*, was published in 2001.

MARY BERRY

Doyenne of home cooking, Mary Berry believes in traditional fare using only fresh ingredients. After training at the Paris Cordon Bleu, Mary started her career as cookery editor of *Housewife* magazine, then moved to *Ideal Home* magazine. She is well known for her cookery with Thames Television and, more recently, for BBC1's *Mary Berry's Ultimate Cakes* and *Mary Berry at Home*. She has often appeared as a guest on the Carlton Food network and for many years was a contributor to the Debbie Thrower programme on BBC Radio 2 and occasional guest on Radio 4's *Woman's Hour*. She has produced her own range of salad dressings and sauces with her daughter Annabel, and has written over 40 cookery books, including *Mary Berry's Ultimate Cakes*, *Mary Berry at Home*, *The AGA Book*, *Mary Berry's New Aga Book*, *Mary Berry's Foolproof Cakes* and *Cook Now, Eat Later*.

CELIA BROOKS BROWN

Celia Brooks Brown left her native Colorado in 1989 for a career directing on the London stage. She rapidly discovered a passion for cooking and transferred her love of entertainment and performance into a career in food. Celia gives live demonstra-

tions all over the UK. She makes regular appearances on the UK Food channel, and wrote and presented her own 25-part series for Taste called *Vegging Out*. She also caters for select clients, including celebrities such as the fashion designer Stella McCartney and TV personality Ruby Wax. Her first major book, *New Vegetarian*, was hailed as 'a gem' by *BBC Good Food* magazine, and is a worldwide success. Her fourth and most recent book, *Entertaining Vegetarians*, was published in September 2003.

GENNARO CONTALDO

Gennaro inherited his passion for food from his parents – his father was a chef and his mother grew her own herbs and plants. As well as helping them in the kitchen, Gennaro spent much of his youth fishing, hunting and picking wild herbs. In 1969 he left his native southern Italy for Britain and worked in restaurants across the country. He then set up an antiques business that involved travelling around the country, allowing him to sample local produce. In the 1980s he teamed up with Antonio Carluccio to help him at his Neal Street restaurant and shop in London, before opening his own restaurant, Passione, in Charlotte Street. Here he once again indulges his love of fresh, natural ingredients by keeping his dishes simple yet full of flavour. His book, *Passione – The Italian Cookbook*, was published in April 2003. He has trained many younger chefs, most notably Jamie Oliver, and has appeared on Jamie's TV programmes as well as on *Saturday Kitchen*.

RICHARD CORRIGAN

Richard Corrigan opened his Michelin-starred Soho restaurant Lindsay House in 1997, where his Celtic origins are evident in a menu of earthy and robust tastes and textures. He started his career at the age of 14 as a trainee chef at the Kirwin Hotel in Co. Meath, Ireland, before moving on to the Kylemore Hotel in Co. Cavan. At 17, he transferred to Holland to further develop his skills, and arrived in London in 1985 at the age of 21 to work with Michel Lorrain at the Meridian Hotel in Piccadilly. In 1994 Richard was awarded his first Michelin star at Stephen Bull's restaurant in Fulham Road. In 1996 he launched Searcy's at the Barbican, London's multi-arts venue. Corrigan's first cookbook, *From the Waters and the Wild*, was published in October 1999.

GINO D'ACAMPO

Gino owns his own company, Bontà Italia, a leading supplier of Italian ingredients to UK food manufacturers. A native of Naples, he developed his passion for food at a young age, helping his grandfather in his restaurant. He graduated with a Master's degree from the Luigi de Medici catering college in Naples in 1995 before gaining further experience in restaurants and hotels in Italy, Spain, Germany and France. He came to England at the end of 1995 and worked in restaurants including the Orchard in Hampstead, the Cambio in Guildford and Mount Royal Charlotte Hotel in Bond Street. His work now involves devising ideas and recipes for products. He regularly visits Italy to find out the latest food trends at the Luigi de Medici college and to visit suppliers to see what's new.

JILL DUPLEIX

Jill Dupleix is the cookery editor of *The Times*, writing a daily column for which she creates simple, straightforward recipes the reader can try at home. Originally from Australia, Jill has travelled widely throughout Southeast Asia and Europe learning about food. She was food editor of the *Sydney Morning Herald* for six years before she and her husband Terry Durack moved to Britain in 2000. Her aim is to encourage cooking that heightens natural flavours – what she calls 'cooking the flavours in, rather than cooking them out'. Jill has written twelve cookery books, the most recent being *Simple Food* and *Very Simple Food*, which feature her own colourful food photography. She was awarded Cookery Writer of The Year in 2002 by the British Guild of Food Writers, and says her recipes suit those who, like her, love to cook – but would rather be eating and drinking.

SILVANA FRANCO

Having enjoyed home-cooked Italian food while growing up in an Italian family, Silvana went on to cook Italian food professionally. While studying at college she completed a work placement at BBC Worldwide where she wrote for *BBC Vegetarian Good Food* magazine and soon progressed to senior writer on its sister magazine, *BBC Good Food*. She later became food editor for *M&S* magazine before moving into the world of television, beginning behind the scenes before switching to front of camera. As well as co-hosting the BBC2 series *The Best*, Silvana has appeared on *GMTV*, *This Morning* and *Good Food Live*. She has written several cookery books, including most recently *Pasta*, *The Best* (co-written with Paul Merrett and Ben O'Donaghue) and in 2003 *Family*. She also helps run Fork, a food media company.

BILL GRANGER

Bill Granger's creative talents went into art before they went into cooking. As an art student in Sydney he worked as a waiter part-time, and before long his focus had moved from art to food. He opened his first restaurant, bills, when he was 22 years old. It soon became an institution and prompted the opening of a second outlet, bills 2, in 1996. His third, billy kwong, soon followed. He has also written two best-selling books, *Sydney Food* and *bills food*. His most recent book, *bills open kitchen*, was published in September 2003.

VALENTINA HARRIS

Valentina specializes in Italian food and culture and runs her own cookery school, Villa Valentina, where students cook in real Italian kitchens in Tuscany. Her most recent books include *100 Great Risottos*, *Al Fresco Cooking* and *Recipes from Villa Valentina*. She has appeared on shows such as *Ready Steady Cook*, *GMTV*, *This Morning* and *Masterchef*, as well as her own series, *Valentina's Italian Regional Cookery*, the book of which was a bestseller. She is also a regular on radio and has written for *BBC Good Food* magazine, *Radio Times*, *Taste*, *The Times* and *The Sunday Times* magazine. She manages her own production company, Edible Creativity, and gives demonstrations and lectures in the UK and abroad. She also acts as a consultant to food manufacturing and retail organizations. She is a member of the International Association of Culinary Professionals.

PAUL HOLLYWOOD

Paul Hollywood is one of Britain's leading bakers, and applies his love of bread-making and sculpting to his cookery appearances. He was head baker at the Dorchester and the Chester Grosvenor, and then after five years as executive head baker at the Annabelle Resort in Cyprus, creating unique and specialized breads and pastries, he returned to Britain and filmed a series, *Use Your Loaf*, with James Martin for the Taste network. He also presented his own series, *Hollywood Loaves*, for the same network. He has appeared on BBC1's *Heaven and Earth* and ITV's *This Morning*, and co-presents *Good Food Live* on UK Food. He opened his own Bread Academy in Canterbury in 2001.

KEN HOM

Ken Hom is widely regarded as one of the world's greatest authorities on eastern cooking and travels extensively to demonstrate his culinary skills. His first UK television series, *Ken Hom's Chinese Cookery*, was broadcast in 1984. It was then transmitted across the world and he has maintained an international reputation ever since. He has made several series for the BBC including *Hot Wok*, *Travels with a Hot Wok* and *Foolproof Chinese Cookery*. His book *Chinese Cookery* has sold over a million copies. He is also author of *Foolproof Thai Cookery*, *Foolproof Asian* and the award-winning *Easy Family Dishes: A Memoir with Recipes*. Ken Hom is a director of Noble House Leisure Limited, which includes the Yellow River Cafés and other restaurants. He also has his own range of woks and accessories.

SUE LAWRENCE

Sue Lawrence is a cookery writer and a regular columnist for *Scotland on Sunday* newspaper and *Scotland* magazine. Originally from Dundee, Sue now lives in Edinburgh, and has also written in recent years for *The Sunday Times*, *Sainsbury's Magazine*, *Country Home and Interiors*, *Country Living*, *Wine Magazine*, *Woman and Home*, *Homes and Gardens* and *Good Housekeeping*. She is also author of 11 cookery books including, most recently, *Scots Cooking* and *Sue Lawrence's Scottish Kitchen*. Sue was the winner of *Masterchef* in 1991 and has won numerous awards, including Glenfiddich Food and Drink Awards Regional Writer 2003, Guild of Food Writers Michael Smith Award 2001 and Guild of Food Writers Recipe Writer of the Year 1998. Sue has also appeared on BBC1's *Good Morning*, BBC2's *Food and Drink*, ITV's *This Morning*, and UK Food's *Good Food Live*.

MANJU MALHI

Manju has her own unique Brit-Indi style of cooking – she uses readily available ingredients to make simple Indian recipes. She won the BBC's *Food and Drink* competition in 1999 and cooked with Antony Worrall Thompson on BBC2. Manju's *Simply Indian* series was aired on the Taste network in early 2001, and her award-winning book, *Brit-Spice*, was published in 2002. She has also appeared on *This Morning*, *Open House* and UK Food's *Good Food Live* as well as *Saturday Kitchen*. She is the face behind Tamarind Fine Foods – a range of gourmet Indian cuisine created by the Michelin-starred restaurant Tamarind. Manju is working on her second book, a British Indian's perspective of what Indians in India eat.

JAMES MARTIN

James's enthusiasm for cooking began as a four-year-old when he helped his father who ran the catering side of Castle Howard. At 16 he began his formal training at Scarborough Technical College where he was Student of the Year for three years running. Antony Worrall Thompson brought him to work in the kitchens of One Ninety Queen's Gate, followed by dell'Ugo. He then travelled throughout Italy and France gaining more culinary experience before moving back to England to work at Chewton Glen for two years. At the age of 22 he opened the Hotel and Bistro du Vin in Winchester as head chef. He now co-owns a successful delicatessen, Cadogan and James, in Winchester and Underwood & James, a bespoke kitchen design company in St Albans. His television career began in 1996 with *Ready Steady Cook* on which he still appears regularly. He has filmed the UK Food series *Delicious* and *Sweet*, is a resident chef on BBC1's daytime show *Housecall* and is presenter of *Use Your Loaf* on ITV. His books include *Great British Dinners*, *Delicious* and *Eating in with James Martin*.

RESHMA MARTIN

Reshma is a Gujarati Indian who was born in Uganda. Her family moved to Wales when she was young and as she grew up she learnt to mix local ingredients with the traditional ones of her background. Although a meat-eater, Reshma, with her vegetarian Gujarati ancestry, believes there is a real diversity to vegetarian food and considers it her job to make it appealing to everyone. Her first appearance on television was when she entered *Chef Star 2002*, run by UK Food's flagship programme *Good Food Live*. She ranked very highly in the competition and is now focusing on inspiring people to experiment and enjoy Indian cuisine in all its diversity.

PAUL MERRETT

Paul Merrett was born on the spice island of Zanzibar, and trained under Gary Rhodes at the Greenhouse in London, following an apprenticeship at the Ritz and three years working with chef Peter Kromberg at Le Soufflé. He then moved to the Terrace Restaurant where he established a reputation for classic modern British cuisine with an Asian twist. His cooking was awarded a Michelin star at Interlude in Charlotte Street, before he returned to the Greenhouse as head chef, where once again he won a Michelin star. Paul has made several TV appearances, including co-presenting BBC2's prime-time series *Fresh Food*, and appearing on *Food Network Daily* on the Taste network. He co-presented a BBC2 prime-time series, *The Best*, with Ben O'Donoghue and Silvana Franco in 2002, which was accompanied by a book of the same name.

MERRILEES PARKER

Merrilees began her career working with a Michelin-trained chef in France before completing a diploma in stage management and technical theatre at LAMDA. After travelling with the Right Size theatre company throughout the UK and a stint at the Edinburgh Fringe, she became a chef at the Lansdowne in Primrose Hill, London. She has worked with Antony Worrall Thompson at his restaurant Wiz (now Notting Grill) and with his restaurant consultancy team, and was also head chef at the Greyhound. Best known for *Anything You Can Cook*, a BBC2 series co-presented with Brian Turner, Merrilees has also been a resident cook on BBC1's *Housecall*. She presents the *Planet Food* series for the Food Network USA, concentrating on the culinary offerings from regions and countries as far apart as

Burgundy, Thailand, Germany, the Caribbean and Brazil. Merrilees owns an event-catering company called Pink Food.

THANE PRINCE

Thane has been professionally involved with food for over 20 years and spent 12 years as cookery columnist for the *Daily Telegraph*. She has been a regular fixture on our television screens (*The Food Programme*, *Junior Masterchef*, *Food and Drink*) and runs a cookery school for enthusiastic amateurs in Aldeburgh, Suffolk. Her most recent television appearances include various programmes for the Carlton Food network and *Home Malone* for Anglia TV. She has written seven books, her most recent being *Simply Good Food*. She contributes regularly to *BBC Good Food* magazine, *Telegraph Magazine* and *Country Living*. She contributes to many radio programmes as well as taking part in food shows including the organization and presentation of the *Telegraph*'s Celebrity Cook's Theatre at Birmingham and London's Good Food Show.

JEANNE RANKIN

Jeanne is from Canada and is one half of the Rankin husband-and-wife team. She met Paul in Greece in the 1980s and they travelled and cooked their way around the world. In 1989 they returned to Belfast to open Roscoff, which earned Northern Ireland its first Michelin star. The couple expanded their chain, restyled as Cayenne, and now have four other cafés and a neighbourhood restaurant called Rain City. Jeanne is a *Ready Steady Cook* regular and has appeared a number of times on BBC2's *Food and Drink* as well as Channel 4's *Light Lunch*. She has appeared with Paul on their series *Gourmet Ireland*, and co-written their numerous books. She was also

recently honoured by her native country as the honorary consul for Canada in Northern Ireland.

PAUL RANKIN

Paul and his wife and fellow-chef Jeanne run the award-winning restaurant Cayenne in Paul's native Belfast. After their culinary world tour, undertaken after they first met in Greece, they worked at the Roux brothers' restaurant, Le Gavroche, in London before doing stints in Canada and California. In 1989 they returned to Belfast to open Roscoff (earner of Northern Ireland's first Michelin star), which was refitted in 1999 to become Cayenne. Paul has appeared on *Masterchef*, *Who'll Do The Pudding?* and *The Good Food Show*. He is a regular on *Ready Steady Cook* and has filmed three series of *The Rankin Challenge* for BBC Northern Ireland. Paul and his wife have published numerous books, the most recent being *New Irish Cookery*.

MIKE ROBINSON

Promotion from dishwasher to chef in a restaurant in the ski resort of Chamonix, France, prompted Mike to learn how to cook classic French food. With this grounding he travelled for another year and a half in Australia where he worked in a top seafood restaurant in Port Douglas and did a stint at a luxury resort in Tasmania. He returned to Bath and set up a deli and catering service to great success. He sold the business in 2000 and went back to France to start a business called SOS Chef. His first foray into television was *Chalet Slaves* for UK Food. He has recently filmed a new TV series for the same channel called *Safari Chef*, in which he samples the local cuisines of Kenya and cooks his way through the country. A further two series are in development.

LIZ SCOURFIELD

Liz's background is in television, with a career that has spanned production management, voiceovers, presenting, sports reporting and children's programmes, and she is currently weather presenter at S4C. Her main passion, however, was always cooking, and she is totally self-taught. She was approached to do a live cookery spot every Wednesday afternoon on S4C Digital and accepted the offer with great pleasure. She has since filmed two pilot food programmes, and is delighted at the turn her career has taken.

CURTIS STONE

Curtis heads his own 45-seater Restaurant 301 in Chelsea, London. He has always loved good food and at the age of 17 decided to make a career of it, starting at the Savoy Hotel in his native Melbourne. After five years working in some of the best kitchens in the city he headed for Europe, spending a summer in Italy before coming to London and the Café Royale under Marco Pierre White. He was soon appointed sous-chef at another Marco Pierre White restaurant, Mirabelle, then a year later Marco promoted him to executive chef at award-winning Quo Vadis. Curtis first appeared on our screens in *Dinner in a Box* for UK TV. His latest series on UK Food, called *Surfing the Menu*, follows him and fellow chef Ben O'Donoghue on their culinary travels throughout Australia. A book of the same name was published in February 2004.

JAMES TANNER

James and his chef brother Christopher own Tanners Restaurant in Plymouth: the fulfilment of a joint life-long ambition. James started his training at the Plough in Kent and then the Bank Street brasserie, before joining his brother at the Greenhills Hotel and then at the Kitley House Hotel in Plymouth. He worked for 18 months at Lake Placid Lodge in upstate New York with the Roux brothers before returning to England to work at the restaurant Lettonie under Martin Blunos. He then became head chef at Right on the Green in Kent. In 1999 James and Christopher took the plunge and opened their restaurant. They both took part in *Chef Star 2002* on UK Food in which they came a close second. James now appears regularly on *Ready Steady Cook*.

TONY TOBIN

Tony has been cooking professionally since the age of 14. After qualifying he cooked in the Chester Grosvenor before moving to London in 1984 to work under Brian Turner at the Capital. He followed this with five years in the Nico Ladenis empire, including Chez Nico in Battersea, Simply Nico and Very Simply Nico. At 25 he took over as head chef at the South Lodge in Lower Beeding, which later won the *Good Food Guide*'s Country Restaurant of the Year, and he is now the chef proprietor at the Dining Room in Reigate, Surrey. He is a regular on BBC2's *Ready Steady Cook*, and has appeared on ITV's *This Morning*, Channel 4's *Light Lunch*, BBC2's *Friends for Dinner*

and *Food and Drink*, as well as presenting three of his own series for the Taste network. Tony now presents regularly on UK Food's live show *Good Food Live*.

MITCH TONKS

Born by the sea, Mitch is passionate about fish. He heads the chain of award-winning seafood restaurants, FishWorks, with business partner Roy Morris. Each venue has independently won a listing in the *Good Food Guide*, and the latest opened in Chiswick, London in 2003. Mitch's first book, *FishWorks Seafood Cafe Book*, was published in November 2001 and shortlisted for the André Simon award. His latest book, *Fresh – Recipes and Advice from a Fish Fanatic*, was published in July 2003. Mitch set up FishWorks Direct, a nationwide home-delivery service, in 2002. He made and presented his own series, called *Fish Food*, for the Carlton Food network in 2001, and has guested on *The Weekend Show*. He has also appeared on UK Food's *Good Food Live* and on Radio 5 Live *Drive Time* offering his superlative advice on fish.

LESLEY WATERS

Lesley studied French cuisine before joining Prue Leith's Restaurant in 1978, where she became senior chef. She later teamed up again with Prue as an instructor at her food and wine school. She has worked in television since 1989, and in addition to *GMTV* and *Bazaar*, her work has included writing and presenting a series of cookery club programmes for Chrysalis TV, and

being resident cook for the Lifestyle Channel and for UK Living. She was also one of the major presenters of *Can't Cook, Won't Cook* and is a *Ready Steady Cook* regular. Guest appearances include BBC's *Food and Drink* and *Who'll Do The Pudding?* She has recorded three of her own series for the Carlton Food network and written a number of cookery books, including *Juice up Your Energy Levels* and *New to Cooking*.

ANTONY WORRALL THOMPSON

Antony Worrall Thompson is the presenter of *Saturday Kitchen*. He has owned many top restaurants in London and now owns Notting Grill in Holland Park. In 1998 he became resident chef for BBC2's *Food & Drink* and he still makes regular appearances on BBC 2's *Ready Steady Cook*. He has also filmed several series for Carlton Food Network including *Worrall Thompson Cooks*, *Simply Antony* and *So You Think You Can't Cook*. He has guested on programmes including *This Morning*, *GMTV* and *Masterchef* as well as *Have I Got News For You*, *Shooting Stars* and *The Kumars at No. 42*. He was a team captain on BBC Radio 4's *Question of Taste* with Oz Clarke and a participant in *I'm A Celebrity, Get Me Out Of Here!* He has also written numerous books, most recently *The Top 100 Recipes from Food & Drink*, *RAW*, *Healthy Eating for Diabetes* and *Well Bred, Well Fed, Well Hung*, a book on meat – and has contributed columns to *The Sunday Times* and *Daily Express*. He currently writes for *The Express on Sunday Magazine* and for Saturday's *Express*.

Who's Who

141

Index